VOLUNTEERING

The Essential Guide

Leonie
Martin

Volunteering – The Essential Guide is also available in accessible formats for people with any degree of visual impairment. The large print edition and eBook (with accessibility features enabled) are available from Need2Know. Please let us know if there are any special features you require and we will do our best to accommodate your needs.

First published in Great Britain in 2011 by
Need2Know
Remus House
Coltsfoot Drive
Peterborough
PE2 9BF
Telephone 01733 898103
Fax 01733 313524
www.need2knowbooks.co.uk

Contents

Introduction

This book is for anyone thinking about volunteering and wondering how and where to start. Written by an author with over 20 years' experience of grass-roots volunteering in a variety of settings, including youth justice, education, health and social care, it will inform and guide you through the basic steps.

From working out the type of role you'll enjoy, to searching for and finding the right organisation and opportunity, this guide also includes plenty of first-hand experiences, plus tips, checklists and contacts to help you take the next step.

Volunteering is a hot topic at the moment. With all the media views about the Big Society, it's easy for the ordinary person to get confused about what volunteering actually means and what it might involve. So many rules and regulations have emerged over recent years that it's easy to be put off. This book explains the essentials without bombarding you with jargon.

Volunteering has a rich history here in the UK – it's been the backbone behind thousands of local and national charities and organisations over the decades. Images traditionally associated with it include uniformed services, wealthy society ladies, students, church-based groups and many, many more.

Volunteering is definitely not a new idea, but the number and type of voluntary opportunities available to us has grown. It's now easier than ever to find a role that will suit you – in person, over the phone or through the Internet.

Volunteers come from hugely diverse backgrounds – don't be put off by outdated myths and stereotypes! This positive mix of people all make a vital contribution in many areas of society, including sport, education, environment, health, social care, arts, animal welfare, culture, leisure.

In today's global economy, fewer families live near each other than in times gone by, resulting in a lack of close support during periods of sickness, family-breakdown and into old age, placing a bigger burden on the state. The services offered by voluntary groups and charities working with both young and elderly people are in more demand than ever before.

'Volunteering has a rich history here in the UK.'

Volunteering can also throw an important lifeline to those living with disability or long-term, limiting illness and who can face difficulties establishing or building independence and identity – it's a great way of building confidence and learning new skills in a less stressful environment, offering a role in the community, without the long-term commitment and pressures of paid work. Many go on to become paid employees as a direct result of volunteering, whilst others gain enormous personal benefits simply from doing what they can, when they can.

Perhaps you are looking for a 'hands-on' role where you can see close up the difference you are making to a particular cause? Or maybe you are more comfortable 'behind the scenes'? You'll be amazed how many different voluntary roles there are.

'Regardless of your background, skills, abilities and ambitions, there'll be a voluntary opportunity out there worth exploring. Go for it!'

This book will act as a signpost to local and national organisations who can help you explore in more detail the latest volunteering opportunities available. Their trained staff will try to ensure that your experience of volunteering is a positive one.

Charities and voluntary groups need reliable and committed volunteers. However, these same organisations are also aware that times have changed over the last decade or so. They are frequently encountering a 'new breed of volunteer'. The modern volunteer is less likely to want to be tied in straight away to any long-term commitment. They are more receptive to short, one-off projects in the first instance to give them a taste of volunteering.

This book will also introduce you to new and exciting types of volunteering that are evolving to meet the time constraints and skills of a new generation. These have developed over the past few decades and include 'virtual volunteering', 'micro-volunteering', 'time-banking' and 'employee volunteering'.

Whatever your reasons for opening this book, there is something else you should know: volunteering is good for you! Studies have shown that volunteering can also have 'a positive effect on volunteers' health' and can impact on many areas including 'longevity, quality of life, self-esteem and sense of purpose', as well as 'reducing depression, stress and pain'.

Regardless of your background, skills, abilities and ambitions, there'll be a voluntary opportunity out there worth exploring. Go for it!

Disclaimer

This book is for general information on volunteering and isn't intended to replace professional advice from volunteer-involving organisations.

All the information in this book was correct at the time of going to press.

Chapter One

What is Volunteering?

Volunteering in times gone by

Fifty years ago, if you had asked a mixed group of people to describe a single image they associated with volunteering, the results would probably have included:

- An elderly lady rattling a collecting tin.

- A uniformed Scout digging a garden.

- A housewife selling home-made cakes at a church fete.

- A lady serving tea in a hospital café.

- A Vicar of Dibley style church council meeting.

Our idea of what a volunteer "looks like" has changed over the years.'

Volunteering in the 21st century

If you were to ask that same question today, the answers would probably be far more varied. In addition to those more traditional images, there might also be descriptions of volunteers taking part in the following roles:

- Running a marathon.

- Giving counselling or advice.

- Listening to a child read in school.

- Abseiling down a viaduct.

- Preparing meals at a homeless shelter for rough sleepers.

- Teaching English to asylum seekers or refugees.

- Planting trees in a park.
- Sorting and pricing donated goods in a charity shop.

Trying to define volunteering

So why do so many people from all walks of life choose to 'donate' free time, energy and skills to a particular cause? Looking at all the above examples, it's easy to see why even the academics find volunteering a difficult concept to define!

In 2010, the Institute of Volunteering Research published a working paper called *A rose by any other name* . . . Revisiting the question: 'what exactly is volunteering?'

This paper defines volunteering as an activity which is:

- Unpaid.
- Undertaken through an act of free will.
- Of benefit to others.

Searches for a new and more 'inclusive' term than volunteering have so far been unable to find an alternative word or phrase that succinctly conveys whatever it is that volunteering is all about. It seems the word 'volunteering' is therefore here to stay – though with an awareness of the continued need to challenge stereotypes and broaden people's understanding of what it encompasses.

Whatever it means, the statistics speak for themselves: a Volunteer England Impact Report published in 2010 stated that in 2008-9, 71% of adults in England volunteered at some point with 47% doing so more than once a month!

Informal volunteering

Most people volunteer at some stage in their lives without even realising it. Anyone giving unpaid help to people who are not relatives, without the involvement of a registered charity or organisation, is considered to be volunteering 'informally'.

Here are some examples of informal volunteering:

- Looking after property or pets.
- Transporting or escorting someone.
- Doing shopping, collecting pension.
- Cooking, cleaning, laundry.
- Decorating, home improvement.
- Babysitting, caring for children.

A report by Volunteer England in 2008 indicated that 67% of the population in England and Wales volunteered informally at least once during the 12 months before interview.

Civic activism

This type of volunteering refers to involvement in direct decision-making about local services, or issues or in the actual provision of these services by taking on a role such as:

- Parish councillor.
- School governor.
- Magistrate.
- NHS Foundation Trust governor.

Views on volunteering

The good . . .

Each of us has our own views on volunteering, formed from our own life-experiences, plus social and family connections. Most will be positive and might be linked to memories of:

- Random acts of kindness from within our own community.
- Practical help and/or emotional support during illness, tragedy or loss.

'A report by Volunteer England in 2008 indicated that 67% of the population in England and Wales volunteered informally at least once during the 12 months.'

- Someone giving their time to teach us a new skill or hobby.
- Practical help and/or emotional support during a domestic crisis.
- A past experience of belonging to a group with a common focus.

Case study

'Two years ago I lost a good friend of mine to cancer. In her last weeks and days she received such wonderful care from our local hospice. I realised how much they rely on volunteers for their fundraising and decided to volunteer one day a week in their local charity shop as my way of saying thank you for all they did. Volunteering has helped me deal with my grief – and helped the hospice too.' Carol, 56.

The bad . . .

It's easy to forget that volunteers and voluntary organisations, just like businesses, are not always perfect. Mistakes and omissions can happen. Sadly, for some people, this may leave a negative image of volunteering which is then passed on to family and friends.

We humans are generally much more likely to remember one negative experience than many of the positive ones that came before it.

Case study

'My grandmother used to clean the premises for a local charity. She went in every weekend for years – to make sure things were right. When she fell ill, nobody from the charity came to visit her. She was really hurt by the whole thing and never went back again.' Tim, 30.

The ugly . . .

When someone in a position of trust is discovered to be a threat to the vulnerable people they are meant to be caring for, the shocking effects are felt right across a community. The outrage is sometimes perceived to be even greater if that person is employed in a voluntary capacity by a charity, faith group and/or working with children or vulnerable adults.

Thankfully, these incidents are few. By comparison, there are countless acts of goodwill carried out by volunteers every day. Unfortunately, these acts of goodwill are much less likely to make the headlines. This can lead to a distorted view of volunteers working in health and social care.

It goes without saying that reasonable arrangements should be in place to reduce the risks posed by a minority of bad people and also by health and safety issues. But with so much negative media attention, there is a real danger that many good people, who at one time would have been prepared to give up their free time, will instead stay at home with their curtains drawn.

If you have been put off volunteering by such negative media coverage, this book will hopefully encourage you to look again and give it another chance.

'If you have been put off volunteering by such negative media coverage give it another chance.'

Changes in volunteering

Times have certainly changed over the last couple of decades in the world of volunteering. Here are just a few of the differences which will be covered in greater detail later in the book:

- It is now much easier to find out about voluntary opportunities.
- The range of roles is much broader.
- Many roles can be carried out flexibly or from home.
- Better training is available for volunteers.
- Volunteers are better supported and managed than in times gone by.

Many voluntary opportunities can now be tailored to fit around our hectic lifestyles, with organisations frequently seeking to fill occasional or one-off voluntary roles. These are also a great way of testing the water to see if you enjoy the experience.

An increasing number of employers are forging links with charities and setting up schemes which enable their employees to volunteer in the local community during work time.

The voluntary and community sector

The voluntary and community sector (VCS) plays an important part in everyday life across the UK. Thousands of organisations of every shape and size are working continuously to improve the lives of local people and communities through a vast range of services and activities.

These organisations are supported by a large workforce of paid staff and unpaid volunteers who provide advice, help, support and resources in areas often missed out by mainstream public and private sector provision.

'The voluntary and community sector (VCS) plays an important part in everyday life across the UK.'

Government support for volunteering

Successive governments have begun to grasp the importance of volunteering, seeing it as a way of making us all a little more caring and helping to create vibrant, inclusive communities.

Reducing red tape

In the Giving White Paper presented to Parliament in May 2011, the government outlines a number of possible strategies intended to reduce red tape and make it easier for volunteers and organisations to find out about voluntary opportunities in their area and give time to charities and community groups.

The paper also acknowledges the limits of government, recognising that volunteering needs to be built from the bottom up, through grass-roots organisations and with opportunities which appeal to people's motivations and interests.

Case study – Red tape

'I've been a nurse all my working life until being made redundant from the hospice I worked at. It was hard to get another job straight away due to recent cutbacks, so I thought about volunteering until paid work came along. Everything I applied for that involved working with people, even just befriending them with a charity, involved so much form filling.

'I was told it would take weeks or even months for all the checks and references even though I'd been working in health for decades. I decided it wasn't worth it as I felt sure I'd find another nursing post within a year – which is exactly what happened. It's a shame – all those months when I was prepared to give my time for nothing, I was stopped by red tape.' Helen, 48.

Celebrating and rewarding volunteers

Volunteers are mostly modest and unassuming characters. They 'do what they do' and are embarrassed when people make a big thing about it.

Having said that, it's important to recognise the massive contribution they make. In the UK, volunteers are a vital part of society, with 22 million volunteers in 2010 contributing to every area of life in the UK. The economic value of volunteering is estimated to be more than £18 billion a year.

There are now designated days and weeks in the year to celebrate those who are involved in volunteering work and to inspire more people to give up their time for free:

- Community Service Volunteers annual 'Make a Difference Day'.
- National Volunteers' Week 1st-7th June each year.
- Student Volunteering Week.

There are as many ways to get involved in volunteering today as there are personalities, skills and circumstances to be accommodated. Volunteering, however you define it, is something that the majority of adults are likely to become involved in, either formally or informally, at some stage of their life. In the process, both they and their communities can only stand to benefit in some way.

'In the UK, volunteers are a vital part of society, with 22 million volunteers in 2010 contributing to every area of life in the UK. The economic value of volunteering is said to be more than £18 billion a year.'

Summing Up

- The word 'volunteering' conjures up a variety of positive or negative images depending on each person's background and life experiences.

- Volunteering is defined as an activity which is unpaid, undertaken through an act of free will and of benefit to others

- In the UK, volunteers are a vital part of society, with 22 million volunteers in 2010 contributing to every area of life in the UK. The economic value of volunteering is estimated to be more than £18 billion a year.

- Successive governments have begun to grasp the importance of volunteering, seeing it as a way of making us all a little more caring and helping to create vibrant, inclusive communities.

- A Volunteer England Impact Report published in 2010 stated that in 2008-9, 71% of adults in England volunteered at some point with 47% doing so more than once a month!

- There are as many ways to get involved in volunteering today as there are personalities, skills and circumstances to be accommodated.

- If you have previously been wary of volunteering, this book will hopefully encourage you to look again and give it another chance.

Need2Know

Chapter Two

Why Volunteer?

If you are reading this book, it is likely that you are already curious about volunteering and what it might involve – you'll want to get stuck in and learn how and where you can start to search for voluntary opportunities. The following chapters will cover all this in detail, but first it's worth spending some time to consider your own individual motivation for volunteering.

Finding the right organisation and role will help to ensure that your first experience of voluntary work will be a positive one that you will enjoy. This chapter will help you to understand where your own motivation stems from and will come in useful when you apply for roles and also once you have found one.

A combination of age, health, ability, social factors, employment status, skills and leisure interests can all contribute to why, how and when to take part in volunteering – as well as past and present influences from family, friends and significant others.

According to a recent Volunteer England Impact Report, most people choose to volunteer at some time in their lives, with 96% of them saying they 'really enjoy it'.

'What is your motivation for volunteering?'

Reasons to volunteer

The most popular reasons why people volunteer can be grouped into six broad headings:

- Improving things/helping people.
- Giving something back.
- Having a say.
- Taking part/spending leisure time.

- Getting to know your community.

- Gaining skills/experience/qualifications for employment.

Improving things/helping people

This is the most popular reason people state for giving up their time for nothing. In fact, according to a 2010 report for Volunteer England, 62% of volunteers started volunteering because they wanted to improve things and/or help people.

It's easy to become disillusioned by today's 24-hour news coverage of the latest crisis, crime or disaster happening somewhere in the world. Watching things unfold on a TV screen can make us feel powerless and frustrated.

Many people are motivated by a desire to improve things in their immediate community or in the wider world. Volunteering can offer them an opportunity to play a small but vital role in improving things for people, animals or the environment.

Improving things for people

Although most of us contribute to the wider society through our taxes, we aren't aware who or what the money is spent on once we have seen it deducted on our pay slip. We have to rely on our democratically elected government to make those decisions on our behalf.

If we want to improve things for people in general or a specific group of people, volunteering offers us a way to do so, without the impact of our efforts being diluted across such a wide range of causes.

If you are motivated by a desire to improve things for people, there are many vital sectors of society where volunteers play a key role, including:

- Advice and counselling.

- Advocacy.

- Children and families.

- Criminal Justice System.

- Disability.

'62% of volunteers started volunteering because they wanted to improve things and/or help people.'

- Education and literacy.
- Elderly health and care.
- Hospitals and health.
- Housing, welfare and addiction.
- Sports and rescue.

Improving things for animals or the environment

With advancements in science and global technology, we are more aware than ever of what is happening around us. But just as animals can't speak for themselves, neither can the environment.

If you are motivated by a desire to improve things for either animals or the environment, there are plenty of ways to volunteer both here in the UK and overseas.

Further information can be found later in the book to help you locate organisations and voluntary opportunities in this field.

Giving something back

Why are so many people motivated to improve things or help people in this way? For many, it's about giving something back.

We can reach a point in our lives when we reflect on who or what has influenced us over the years:

- A family member or friend who was there when we needed them.
- A sports coach or teacher who saw our potential and encouraged us.
- A health professional that went the extra mile to make sure we received the best medical treatment.

The list is endless – unique to each person – but the desire to give something back to 'society' is something many of us have in common. It's often referred to as 'karma'.

Volunteering can enable you to fulfill this desire, yet at the same time benefit someone or something else. It's a perfect way to pass on the kindness or inspiration that you yourself received.

Giving something back to a particular cause

Most people who decide to volunteer for the first time are motivated by a particular cause that has influenced them, or someone they have known, just as people putting money in a collection box at a supermarket are likely to put more money in if the collection is for a cause close to their heart.

If this is you, you will probably find that what you get back from your voluntary role is worth far more than the time you put into it. It's important to remember though, that feeling strongly about a cause can sometimes mean that we over-commit ourselves. Advice on how to avoid this is given later in the book.

'Most people who decide to volunteer for the first time are motivated by a particular cause that has influenced them.'

Case study

'I used to be a builder until I badly injured my back. The spinal injuries unit was fantastic with me. Although I knew I'd never be able to go back to my job, they helped to get me back on my feet, and regain my independence.

'I'd always enjoyed reading crime fiction and wondered about having a go at writing stories. I joined a local writing group and contributed to a prize-winning anthology of short stories which was sold to raise money for a spinal injuries unit. It was an amazing feeling seeing my work in print and benefitting others at the same time!' Paul, 58.

Giving something back to society in general

For some people, the particular cause they give their time isn't so important. They might prioritise their search for a voluntary role by whatever fits around their skills and lifestyle. In their own mind, they are able to remember how it felt to receive help and can use that personal connection to help them stay motivated in their volunteering role.

Not everyone volunteers purely because they want to give something back. For some, the motivation to improve things/help people is combined with the desire to 'have a say' in some aspect of their community.

'Having a say'

Having a say in your local community

Some people want more than the opportunity to vote at general elections, and decide to vote with their feet by becoming involved in local community, neighborhood and citizens' groups where they can express their views and contribute skills and experience to matters closer to home.

This type of volunteering includes volunteer representatives in parish councils and local authorities and school governors. As explained in chapter 1, this is formally referred to as 'civic activism'. But don't be put off by this heavy-sounding title! Chapter 4 of this book provides information about these vital and rewarding community roles.

Having a say in the wider community

Over recent years, campaigning and activism have become another popular form of volunteering for some people. This is in part due to access to the Internet and its blogs and discussion forums which have encouraged debates about political and social issues. Some well-known examples are the Countryside Alliance, the anti-war movement, the Make Poverty History campaign and the Green movement.

Enjoying quality leisure time

Volunteering offers a chance to take part in activities that can be completely different to our other roles. This contrast can help to balance our lifestyle and make us happier and more well-rounded adults. Here are some examples:

'Volunteering offers a chance to take part in activities that can be completely different to your other roles.'

- A call center operator can also be a special constable.
- A sales manager can also be a football coach.
- A physiotherapist can also be a street pastor.
- An accountant can also be a youth mentor.
- An unemployed person can work in a charity shop.

Taking part in a shared hobby or interest

Many people volunteer without even realising it – they are too busy enjoying taking part! It's just who they are and how they choose to spend their spare time.

These volunteers play an essential role in many areas of society, including:

- Animal welfare.
- Arts and heritage.
- Education and literacy.
- Faith groups.
- Sports and rescue.

Case study

'I began volunteering as a way of combining my love of football with family time at the weekends. I've been managing my son's football team for seven years now – it's been a privilege watching the lads grow up, having fun and improving their skills. My job involves a lot of sitting down, driving, flying and in meetings so it's a great way for me to be outdoors and stay fit too!' Craig, 48.

Spending time with family or friends

With most people working ever longer hours during the week, volunteering offers families and groups of friends or neighbours an increasing range of opportunities for sharing quality leisure time. By volunteering, kids learn the importance of helping others and get to try something new, and adults enjoy a fun, free activity for all the family.

Useful tip

CSV Annual Make a Difference Day

Every autumn the UK volunteering charity CSV runs the nation's biggest single day of volunteering. CSV Make a Difference Day is the perfect opportunity to get 'stuck in', make friends, get fit, spend time with the family and get to know the neighbours. In 2010 more than 70,000 people took part, making a positive impact on a huge range of causes that included helping premature babies, through to creating homes for snakes, bees and newts, and protecting ancient burial mounds.

For further information go to www.csv.org.uk and click on 'campaigns' then 'csv-make-difference-day'. Here you will find information on how to get involved at an event in your local community and be able to sign up to the CSV newsletter.

Getting to know your community

Studies have shown that as a nation we spend an increasing amount of our free time watching television, playing electronic games and keeping in touch with the outside world via computers and mobile phones.

When we are out at work for most of the week, there isn't the same incentive to find out what's happening in our community.

If there are school age children in the house then we regularly come into contact with other families. But if, or when, our circumstances change and we find ourselves spending more time at home, it can be much harder to adjust if we are isolated from our community.

'In 2010 more than 70,000 people took part in the CSV Make a Difference Day.'

A change of circumstances can happen to us at any age and for a variety of reasons, including:

- Bereavement.
- Change of health/disability.
- Children growing up/leaving home.
- Redundancy.
- Relationship breakdown.
- Relocation.
- Retirement.

It's normal to feel anxious or doubt your abilities when you have experienced changes in your life, and volunteering can help to rebuild your confidence and self-esteem. It offers the chance to try out new skills or opportunities in a less formal or demanding setting, to meet new people and even discover parts of your town or community you never knew existed!

Benefits of volunteering in the community

If you have been affected by any of these changes, volunteering can offer you a way to meet new people and learn more about the community. It can also help you in many other ways, including:

- Escaping negative feelings.
- Boosting your confidence.
- Staying active.
- Learning new skills.
- Having fun.
- Adapting to your changed situation.

Need2Know

Case studies

'When I retired I needed something to keep me active, physically and mentally. I've been the volunteer treasurer for a local health charity for three years now. I've been able to keep my financial and IT skills up to date, as well as meet a whole new group of people.' Sue, 63.

'I used to be medical secretary but had to retire early after complications with my diabetes. Then we moved to a different part of the country where I hardly knew anyone. I volunteered for 5 years as the secretary of my local diabetes group – it helped me keep my skills up to date as well getting to know a whole new community.' Jane, 58.

For those whose health, age or circumstances mean it is unlikely they'll be able to return to paid work, volunteering can also benefit in many ways, including:

- Providing a manageable sense of purpose or routine.
- Meeting new people in a community setting.
- Retaining old skills.
- Learning new skills.

Health benefits to community volunteering

Evidence suggests that volunteering brings health benefits to both volunteers and the people they help.

In an attempt to measure this positive effect on volunteers, Volunteering England recently commissioned the University of Wales to undertake a review of research on the subject. The review reported that health benefits of volunteering can include:

- A longer life.
- Ability to cope with ill health.
- A healthier lifestyle.
- Improved family relationships.

'Evidence suggests that volunteering brings health benefits to both volunteers and the people they help.'

- Meeting new people.

- Improved self-esteem and sense of purpose.

- A positive view of your own health.

Useful tip
For further information on this review, go to www.nhs.uk and click on 'livewell', then 'volunteering', then 'why volunteer'. Here you will find all the information about this review with personal experiences from NHS volunteers.

Gaining job skills, knowledge and experience

It is commonly said to be 'easier to find work when you already have a job'. But if you are someone for whom the odds of finding employment have been stacked against you by circumstances beyond your control, this type of statement will only add to your frustration!

There are some groups of people for whom this situation is often a reality:

- Students and young people.

- People with a disability.

- People with life-limiting conditions.

- Ex-offenders.

- Refugees and asylum seekers.

Students and young people

Students and young people stand a much higher chance of employment if they have work experience on their CV – in fact many students are required to volunteer in a relevant setting as part of their course requirements.

Case study

'As part of my social work degree, I volunteered at a residential facility with people who had physical and mental health disabilities, and also at a care home for the elderly. It helped me to realise where my strengths lie. I now know I'm better suited to working with older people and now that I have qualified have found the right career.' Arlette, 23.

People with a disability or life-limiting condition

A recent study carried out on behalf of the government's Office for Civil Society revealed that the experience of being in a working environment increased confidence and improved employment prospects for disabled volunteers.

For further information on volunteering for people with a disability go to www.do-it.org.uk and click on 'want to volunteer', then 'about volunteering' and then 'disabilities'.

'Volunteering can help you rebuild your confidence, maintain a routine, learn new skills or even try out a new profession.'

Case study

'I found it hard to get work after being diagnosed with multiple sclerosis, and decided to volunteer as website editor for my local MS branch. It helped me to feel part of the community again and my confidence improved. The charity was able to supply me with a reference, and I eventually found a paid job with a media company. Volunteering was a great stepping stone back to paid employment.' Ed, 30.

If you are finding it difficult to get paid employment, volunteering can help you to improve your job prospects and employability by:

- Gaining new skills, knowledge and experience.

- Developing existing skills and knowledge.

- Gaining an accreditation.

- Enhancing your CV.
- Gaining confidence and self-esteem.
- Gaining insight into a profession.

Possible restrictions

Although certain restrictions apply in some areas of volunteering – we'll look at these later in this book – with so many types of volunteering opportunities available, there is something to suit everyone.

Ex-offenders

If you have recently left prison, volunteering could be the vital route into employment, as it could help you to update skills, or use any new ones developed while in prison through education and training programmes. It could also give you the confidence to apply for jobs and give you someone to put down as a referee on your CV.

Refugees

People with refugee status (or those who have exceptional leave to remain) can volunteer and claim out of pocket expenses. This might mean they are in a better position to get work if their claim is accepted. Volunteering for an organisation in an area of interest could offer training, practical experience and the chance to network.

Staying active between jobs

The days of having a 'job for life' are long gone. Few people will remain with the same employer for the bulk of their working life. At some stage, many of us will find ourselves 'between jobs'. This might be the result of economic factors or personal circumstances, but either way, it can be a huge shock both financially and emotionally.

The current economic situation is likely to mean that people who might previously never have thought about volunteering will now consider it whilst they search for paid work.

Volunteering can offer useful benefits to people who find themselves between jobs. These can include:

- Rebuilding confidence.
- Maintaining a routine.
- Learning new skills.
- The chance to try out a new profession.

Case study

'I started driving for my local community transport department after I suffered a heart attack and was made redundant from my long-standing job in engineering. I'd always worked, so I hated being at home with nothing to structure my day around. Although I had to keep an eye on my health after my heart attack, I felt well and missed chatting to people. I kept visiting the Job Centre but there didn't seem to be anything for me. I was either the wrong age or didn't have the right skills.

'When I heard they needed volunteer drivers for the local community transport bus I jumped at the chance. I've been driving with them for 3 years now and it's been great for me – I enjoy driving and have met some wonderful people. A paid driving position came up and I was invited to apply for it – the fact that I had volunteered first stood me in good stead and I was successful.

'If ever I was made redundant again I'd volunteer. It's given me a whole new lease of life and I'd recommend volunteering to anyone who finds themselves between jobs. You never know where it might lead, and in the meantime you'll enjoy the sense of achievement it gives you.' Kevin 54.

Gaining qualifications

What is accreditation?

Accreditation is the formal recognition of the achievements of an individual, linked up to some internal or external standard. In other words, it is a process of confirming that someone's performance conforms to standards that are agreed or approved.

Some organisations may offer volunteers qualifications such as an NVQ. You may also be able to keep a record or portfolio that would help you get a qualification or entry to a college course.

Case study

'I volunteer because it's my community and I want to give something back. Every moment with such a supportive team of volunteers has been memorable, and getting my recent OCN Level 2 Qualification in 'Supporting Families' was a huge achievement. We celebrated at an event where certificates were presented in front of the volunteers' families and friends.' Nicola, Family Support Volunteer, Action for Children.

Why do you want to volunteer?

So far in this chapter we have looked at common reasons why people volunteer and highlighted some of the additional benefits that can be experienced.

It's important to think carefully about why you, personally, want to volunteer and how you hope to benefit. Use the chart below to help you, by ticking any number of the reasons listed that might apply to you.

This chart will come in useful as we move on to the next chapter and begin to explore some of the different sorts of volunteer roles. It will also be useful to have this information for any future volunteer application forms or interviews.

Your reason/s for volunteering . . .	☑
Improving things for people	
Improving things for animals or the environment	
Giving something back to a particular cause	
Giving something back to society in general	
Having a say in the local community	
Having a say in the wider community	
Taking part in a shared hobby or interest	
Spending time with family or friends	
Getting to know your community	
Gaining job skills, knowledge and experience	

Summing Up

- Most people that decide to volunteer for the first time are motivated by a particular cause that has influenced them, or someone they have known.

- A combination of age, health, ability, social factors, employment status, skills and leisure interests can all contribute to why, how and when to take part in volunteering – as well as past and present influences from family, friends and significant others.

- The majority of volunteers started volunteering because they wanted to improve things and/or help people

- For some, the motivation to improve things/help people is combined with the desire to 'have a say' in some aspect of their community.

- Many people volunteer without even realising it – they are too busy enjoying taking part!

- It's normal to feel anxious or doubt your abilities when you have experienced changes in your life, and volunteering can help to rebuild your confidence and self-esteem.

- Evidence suggests that volunteering brings health benefits to both volunteers and the people they help.

- If you are finding it difficult to get paid employment, volunteering can help you to improve your job prospects and employability.

Chapter Three

Where do I Start?

In the previous two chapters we have looked at reasons why people volunteer, along with some of the additional benefits this can bring for themselves, their community and the UK economy.

We are all unique, with different life experiences, personalities and skills that we can bring to a voluntary role. In this chapter, we are going to introduce some guidelines and tips to help you find a voluntary role to fit around you and your lifestyle.

There are three important areas you need to consider before going any further:

- What matters to me?
- How much time can I spare?
- What can I do?
- What type of role will I enjoy?

Let's break these down and look at each one in more detail.

'Your time is a precious commodity! If you are looking to "donate" your time to a cause, it makes sense to find one that matters to you personally.'

What matters to me?

Your time is a precious commodity! If you are looking to 'donate' your time to a cause, it makes sense to find one that matters to you personally, otherwise you may find it hard to stay motivated.

Connecting with a cause

Many people are drawn into volunteering through an interest in a particular 'cause' such as sport, music, education, faith, welfare, animals, the environment or politics.

Parents of young children can find it easier to get involved in community projects because of the involvement of their own child. They are happy to give up free time for a cause through which the whole family can benefit.

Students and young people often have to undertake relevant voluntary work as part of their training but go on to form lasting ties with a particular cause or organisation.

If none of the above applies to you, the following prompts might help you to understand the causes you connect with:

- When you watch TV, read the paper or listen to the news, do you find yourself having strong opinions about any current media topics? There's usually something that makes us want to climb up on our soap box! Volunteering is a great way of doing something positive about it.

- Have you, a member of your family, a friend or colleague ever been affected by a health condition or trauma? These days there are many local and national health and medical charities along with related support groups who are always on the lookout for regular and one-off volunteers.

- Is your job office-based? Would you like to have a go at something outdoors in your free time and get fit in the process?

- Have you previously had a hobby or interest that you gave up due to changes in your employment, family circumstances or any other reason, but would now like to be involved with again?

- Do you live in an urban area but want to get closer to nature? Volunteering can give you the opportunity to work with animals or on the land within your home city.

- Do you live in a rural area? In large rural counties, much of the population lives in relatively isolated locations, where there can be 'pockets' of severe deprivation. As well as opportunities within health and social care, volunteering can offer you a way to learn about rural conservation and heritage.

How much time can I spare?

Think carefully about your time before making enquiries about voluntary opportunities. Most of us already have family, work or study commitments and it is very easy to over-commit yourself which will spoil your enjoyment of volunteering.

When are you free?

It's a good idea to write down the hours or days you are usually free. Most people's routines can change with the time of year or as other commitments come and go. To begin with, try and work around your typical week at the moment without thinking too far ahead. Use the chart below to help you with this:

Day	Morning		Afternoon		Evening	
	From	To	From	To	From	To
Monday						
Tuesday						
Wednesday						
Thursday						
Friday						
Saturday						
Sunday						

'Think carefully about your time before making enquiries about voluntary opportunities.'

Useful tips

- Have this chart and the chart from chapter 2 handy when you discuss any volunteering opportunities over the phone, Internet or face-to-face.

- If you are new to volunteering it might be best to begin with a one-off project or just a few hours per week/month and build up from there.

- Don't make long-term commitments to volunteering unless you are sure you can fit them around your work, studies or family obligations.

I'm already working full-time

The good news is that an increasing number of employers are beginning to notice the positive impact volunteering has on the wellbeing of their employees as well the wider benefit in their communities. Many are setting up their own 'employee schemes' that can be run during the working day.

In addition to this, most volunteer-involving organisations don't keep nine-to-five hours and work as far as possible around the needs of their volunteers – it is in their interests to be as flexible as possible if they want to recruit and retain good volunteers!

What can I do?

As well as finding a cause or interest that motivates you and deciding how much time you can comfortably give to it, it's just as important to think about the sorts of role that will suit you as an individual.

Most charities need a wide range of volunteers in many different roles. Some people try several different voluntary roles within different organisations before finding the right one.

Here are some prompts to help you with this thinking process – have a pen and paper handy to jot down the first things that come into your head in response to each one.

- What am I good at?
- What will I enjoy?
- What previous experience do I have?
- How much responsibility do I want?

Now let's look at each of these in more detail so that you can add to any notes you have made.

What are you good at?

Many people are modest and tend to underplay their positive qualities. Sometimes it's easier for others to spot things we take for granted about ourselves. Try asking someone who knows you well where they think your strengths lie.

Has anyone ever commented that you have a particular talent or skill? It doesn't have to be creative – it can be sporty, technical, practical or anything at all. Perhaps you've been told you are a good listener? Can you make people smile? Are you a competent driver?

Are you a people person or more comfortable behind the scenes? Do you prefer talking or listening – or are you equally comfortable with both?

Are you a practical, hands-on person or more comfortable with paperwork and planning?

Your previous experience

Spend a moment thinking about the different roles you have experienced up to now – you'll be surprised how many you can come up with if you include informal roles as well as the obvious formal ones. Which of these roles came most naturally to you? These will tend to be the ones you are good at.

Formal roles

Each of us will have many different roles over the course of a lifetime. Some of these are easy to name because they relate to a past or present type of employment. These are our 'formal' roles and we are generally much better at recognising and remembering them and the skills and experience we gained through them.

Informal roles

We tend to overlook the skills and experiences gained through 'informal' roles within our circle of family, friends and neighbours, as well as through hobbies or community groups we have been involved with in the past. These roles and the skills we learnt in them can be just as useful as the formal ones.

'Many people are modest and tend to underplay their positive qualities.'

What will I enjoy?

Volunteering should be enjoyable. If it isn't, you'll easily lose your motivation. Think about the sort of things you enjoy. Here are a few prompts to help you:

- Indoor or outdoor activities?
- Sport or the arts?
- Working as part of a group or one-to-one?
- Working from home or at a different location?
- Talking or listening?
- Front of house or behind the scenes?
- Working with people or animals?

How much responsibility do you want?

Even though voluntary work is unpaid, it still requires a whole range of people who work at different levels of responsibility.

It's important that you think about levels of responsibility when making enquiries with a charity so that you understand exactly how much of it a potential voluntary role involves.

These days, most voluntary opportunities have a job description outlining the duties involved, and organisations offer training and regular supervision when you can raise any concerns you have about your potential or existing voluntary role.

Be aware of your limitations

Some people thrive on responsibility and are happy to make decisions and organise people, events and procedures. Others can become anxious and unhappy if placed in voluntary roles which have added responsibility. That doesn't mean their voluntary role is any less important – just that their strengths lie in a different direction.

Useful tip

Grab a pen and paper, spend a few moments thinking about the following questions and jot down your responses:

- How do you cope under pressure?
- Are you someone who needs regular reassurance and appreciation for what you do?
- Are you happier when left to get on with things?

Summing Up

- Your time is a precious commodity! If you are looking to 'donate' your time to a cause, it makes sense to find one that matters to you personally.

- Many people are drawn into volunteering through an interest in a particular 'cause' such as sport, music, education, faith, welfare, animals, the environment or politics.

- Think carefully about your time before making enquiries about voluntary opportunities.

- Don't make long-term commitments to volunteering unless you are sure you can fit them around your work, studies or family obligations.

- An increasing number of employers are beginning to notice the positive impact volunteering has on the wellbeing of their employees, as well the wider benefit in their communities.

- Sometimes it's easier for others to spot things we take for granted about ourselves. Try asking someone who knows you well where they think your strengths lie.

- Volunteering should be enjoyable. If it isn't, you'll easily lose your motivation. Think about the sort of things you enjoy.

- Think about levels of responsibility when making enquiries with a charity, so that you understand exactly how much of it a potential voluntary role involves.

Chapter Four

Types of Voluntary Role

These days, there are voluntary opportunities to suit everyone and anyone. In fact, there are so many that it can sometimes be difficult to decide where to begin!

In this chapter, we are going to introduce some different types of voluntary role commonly found within local and national organisations in the UK. By comparing this information with what you have learnt in the previous chapters, you'll be well equipped to move on to the next stage – searching and applying for a voluntary opportunity that's right for you.

'These days, there are voluntary opportunities to suit everyone and anyone.'

'Front line' roles in the community

If it's important for you to connect, face-to-face, with the cause or interest you are supporting, there are lots of typical voluntary roles where you can do so.

These can be broken into five categories:

- Listening, signposting and representing.
- Helping out.
- Educating and inspiring.
- Fundraising.

Let's look at each of these in turn and the ways volunteers can contribute to them.

Listening, signposting and representing

If your previous roles, either formal or informal, have required you to be patient, non-judgemental and a good listener, you will know if this comes naturally to you. If it does, you might be suited to one of the following roles:

- Advocacy – speaking up for and representing others in need.
- Befriending and 'buddying'.
- Caring.
- Counselling.
- Educational speaking.
- Mentoring.

Helping out

If you are a practical or hands-on person, with experience in a specific field, here are just a few of the typical voluntary roles found in different organisations.

- Catering.
- Cleaning and domestic help.
- Driving.
- First aid.
- Gardening.
- Practical work and DIY.

Useful tip

Many hospitals have a Voluntary Services Manager who will be able to advise you on current volunteering opportunities. Call your local NHS Trust for more information.

Educating and inspiring

If you have a particular profession, skill or talent and would like to use it in volunteering, there is always a need for volunteers in the following areas:

- Arts and music and entertainment.
- Heritage and environment sites.
- Sport and outdoor activities.
- Teaching, training and coaching.

Fundraising

This is literally the 'bread and butter' of most charities, particularly the small local ones that receive little or no extra funding. Fundraising is often the most flexible way to volunteer. Depending on the size of a charity, they usually raise funds in a variety of ways

Helping in charity shops

Many larger charities have a national network of shops where donated goods are sold to raise vital funds. No special skills are required, just a willingness to help. Typical roles in charity shops include:

- Till work.
- Stock control.
- Sorting donations.
- Window display.

Helping with store and street collections

Charities need volunteers to help at local supermarket collections, or by placing pin badges or collection boxes in local businesses. This might typically include the following roles:

'Fundraising is literally the "bread and butter" of most charities.'

- Co-ordinating other volunteers.
- Setting up and clearing away.
- Taking a turn at collecting.

Helping with fundraising events

Many local charities hold regular fundraising events in the community and need volunteers to help with:

- Co-ordinating other volunteers.
- Selling raffle tickets and displaying posters.
- Donating prizes for raffles and tombolas.
- Manning stalls.
- Setting up and clearing away.

Helping at or taking part in sponsored challenges

Sponsored challenges have increased in popularity over the last decade with a whole range of indoor and outdoor events now taking place all year across the country and abroad. From running and walking, to bathing in a tub of baked beans, having your head shaved or walking the Pennine Way – the list is endless!

These events usually take place in the evenings or at weekends and volunteers are needed for many in essential roles, including:

- Registering participants.
- Marshalling a course.
- Giving out water.

'Behind the scenes' voluntary roles

Are you more comfortable working behind the scenes? Do you have a demanding career or a life-limiting condition or disability which prevents you from taking on certain activities? Don't worry – there are many flexible volunteering opportunities.

Many of these can be done from home or at a designated office space.

Every registered charity must have a committee to manage its business. There is always a demand for volunteers to fill the various committee posts. Even small charities will need a chairperson, secretary, treasurer, with most also having a range of behind the scenes roles in membership, information, publications and media.

Volunteering behind the scenes requires just as much commitment, but you can often tailor the role to suit your circumstances. It's important to have a strong affinity with the particular cause you are working for – it will help to keep you motivated in your vital but unobtrusive place behind the scenes!

Never feel that volunteering from behind the scenes is a lesser role. It's the oil that keeps the machine from grinding to a halt! Here are just a few of the vital roles volunteers are involved in:

- Committee work and trusteeship.
- Health and safety administration.
- Accounts and administration.
- Business management and research.
- Campaigning and lobbying.
- Computers, technology and website design.
- Marketing, PR and media.
- Events planning and co-ordinating.

Increasingly, the Internet is enabling many more people to become involved in behind the scenes roles.

'Every registered charity must have a committee to manage its business.'

Helping in the Criminal Justice System

This type of voluntary work is demanding and requires specific skills, abilities, checks and training, but will almost certainly challenge some of your pre-conceptions about victims of crime, young offenders, prisoners, prisoners' families, prisons, and the people who work in them.

Here are some of the ways in which people can volunteer in the Criminal Justice System:

- Becoming a magistrate.
- Becoming a special police constable.
- Becoming a police support volunteer.
- Mentoring young people at risk of offending.
- Supporting victims of crime.
- Supporting witnesses giving evidence in court.
- Helping people in prison and immigration removal centres.

Volunteering as a school or college governor

'Anyone aged 18 or over can become a school governor.'

Becoming a governor is a rewarding way of making an important contribution to education. It can help you develop your existing skills and learn new ones.

Anyone aged 18 or over can become a school governor. No specialist qualifications are needed and people from many different backgrounds volunteer for the role. Enthusiasm, commitment and an interest in education are the most important qualities. You don't need to have a family member attending a school or college to become a governor.

As a school or college governor, your duties will include:

- Setting the strategic direction, policies and objectives.
- Approving the budget.
- Reviewing progress against the budget and objectives.
- Challenging and supporting senior staff.
- Playing a part in appointing staff.

For more information about becoming a school governor, go to www.direct.gov.uk and click on 'home and community', then 'getting involved in your community', then 'volunteering as a school or college governor'.

Volunteering in your child's school

There are several different ways you can volunteer at your child's school including:

- Listening to pupils read.
- Joining school trips.
- Helping with drama productions.
- Helping with one-off events.
- Sharing relevant skills as part of the curriculum.

If you are interested in volunteering, talk to your child's teacher or the head teacher at their school. You will need to have a police background check before you can start.

New and different ways to volunteer

Green volunteering

'Green volunteering' is a way of working for organisations that make a positive environmental difference to your community. By taking small steps locally, you can make a big environmental difference globally.

These small, local steps include getting involved with:

- Local wildlife conservation initiatives.
- Supporting environmental education projects.
- Recycling.

To find out more about greener living and the Big Tree Plant scheme go to www.direct.gov.uk and click on 'home and community', then 'getting involved in your community', then 'green volunteering and working with animals'.

Volunteering to work with animals

Volunteering activities available for people who want to work with animals include:

- Dog walking and kennel duties.
- Looking after injured animals.
- Working at local community farms.
- Monitoring local wildlife.
- Working with stray and feral cats.
- Helping out at the local zoo.

Before volunteering your time, you should think about the level of commitment you are willing to provide. Looking after animals can be hard, physical work and you may need some training.

Most animal rescue centres won't expect you to be an animal specialist. However, a love of animals and the desire to learn more about them will help.

For more information about volunteering to work with animals, go to www.direct.gov.uk and click on 'home and community', then 'getting involved in your community', then 'green volunteering and working with animals'.

Residential volunteering

Residential volunteering offers the chance to try things for a week or two or to dedicate a year or even longer to working with an organisation, living away from home. Opportunities exist in a range of organisations, including environmental and conservation groups, care organisations and animal welfare. Faith-based organisations can also be an important source of residential opportunities.

For further information about residential volunteering go to www.volunteering.org.uk and click on 'resources', then 'good practice bank', then 'information' from where you will be able to download an information sheet.

Volunteering outside the UK

Volunteering opportunities available in the rest of the world are as diverse as those available in the UK. It's therefore a good idea to consider very carefully the sort of activity you want to do, your reasons for doing it and the resources available to you before you start looking for an opportunity.

'Before volunteering your time, you should think about the level of commitment you are willing to provide.'

Opportunities arranged from the UK come in a variety of forms, with the most common being:

- Professional volunteering for at least a year, which typically covers the cost of flights, accommodation and subsistence.
- Non-professional volunteering for anything from a few weeks to a year, for which volunteers will usually have to fundraise or contribute financially.
- Time-limited fundraising challenges.

It is best to apply well in advance. Not all projects are well organised, so it's a good idea to find out as much as you can beforehand. If possible, speak with volunteers who have returned from the project to find out how they found it.

It is also possible to travel to a country and then find voluntary work. However, you should check first if your visa allows volunteering and bear in mind that it can take many weeks to be selected on to a volunteer programme.

For further information on volunteering outside the UK go to www.volunteering.org.uk and click on 'resources', then 'good practice bank', then 'information' from where you will be able to download an information sheet.

Volunteering through sport

Sports clubs provide the best opportunities to offer volunteer help to your favourite sport. Volunteer roles include coaching, administration, refereeing, driving and management.

Sport England has a Sports Gateways online database of local and national sporting contacts. For further information go to www.sportengland.org.

English Federation of Disability Sport works to increase and improve opportunities for disabled people in sport. It has a range of volunteering opportunities through its regional and event networks. For further information go to www.edfs.co.uk.

Micro-volunteering

Micro-volunteering is about doing small, short-term voluntary actions that benefit a good cause, usually in less than 30 minutes.

'Micro-volunteering is about doing small, short-term voluntary actions that benefit a good cause, usually in less than 30 minutes.'

Help from Home provides information on over 500 micro-volunteering actions/ initiatives that can all be done in a short period of time from your own home. Web: http://www.helpfromhome.org.

Orange has launched a micro-volunteering initiative called 'Do Some Good'. It's an app that lets people do bite-size actions on their mobile in five minutes or less, making micro-volunteering easy. There are 12 charitable actions – from completing a charity survey to taking wildlife photos. www.orange.co.uk/dosomegood.

For more information about micro-volunteering go to www.volunteering.org.uk and click on 'I want to volunteer', then 'what can I do'.

TimeBank

For people who know their time and skills are in demand, but do not know where to begin, the best place to start is the national charity TimeBank. It provides people with the inspiration, opportunities and support to volunteer.

TimeBank constantly develops new and exciting ways to involve volunteers and its projects address very real needs. People who register with TimeBank have access to an online chat forum where they can get all their volunteering questions answered.

For further information go to www.timebank.org.uk.

Employer-supported volunteering

More businesses are starting to offer their workers the chance to volunteer through company projects. This is known as employer-supported volunteering (ESV) and can include projects such as:

- Running a mentoring scheme at a local school – which can be fitted in during lunchtime or at the beginning of the day.

- One-off 'challenge events' such as refurbishing a youth club or spending an evening helping to tidy a communal area outside the office.

ESV often forms part of an organisation's Corporate Social Responsibility (CSR) Policy. In ESV schemes, employers encourage their employees to get involved in their local communities by volunteering their time, their skills or both.

There are three main ways in which employers promote community involvement amongst their staff:

- Companies operate an ESV scheme in which a dedicated member of staff proactively identifies and develops volunteering opportunities with local voluntary and community organisations. Employees can volunteer during working hours, whilst not incurring any financial penalties.

- Employees are encouraged to find their own volunteering opportunities within the community, and are given the flexibility to fit their work around the volunteering opportunity. In some schemes, employees can take sabbaticals, whilst others volunteer on an ongoing, regular basis.

- Employees enable voluntary and community organisations to benefit from their business skills and experience. Such employees may undertake pro bono work, provide voluntary consultancy services, or serve as trustees.

For more information on employer-supported volunteering schemes contact your local volunteer centre or go to www.volunteering.org.uk and click on 'resources', then 'good practice bank', then 'specialist themes'.

'ESV often forms part of an organisation's Corporate Social Responsibility (CSR) Policy.'

Summing Up

- These days, there are voluntary opportunities to suit everyone and anyone. In fact, there are so many that it can sometimes be difficult to decide where to begin!

- If it's important for you to connect, face-to-face, with the cause or interest you are supporting, there are lots of typical voluntary roles where you can do so.

- Fundraising is literally the 'bread and butter' of most charities, particularly the small local ones that receive little or no extra funding. Fundraising is often the most flexible way to volunteer.

- If you are a practical or hands-on person, with experience in a specific field such as gardening, driving, catering etc. there is always a demand for volunteers with practical skills.

- Volunteering in the Criminal Justice System is demanding and requires specific skills, abilities, checks and training, but will almost certainly challenge some of your pre-conceptions.

- Never feel that volunteering from behind the scenes is a lesser role. It's the oil that keeps the machine from grinding to a halt!

- There are many new and different ways to volunteer today, including sport, green volunteering and working with animals, residential volunteering, micro-volunteering, TimeBank and employer-supported volunteering.

Chapter Five

Searching for a Voluntary Role

Once you've thought about why you want to volunteer, found a cause that motivates you, and have an idea of the sort of role that will suit you, it's time to make contact and get involved.

Although it is much easier today to find out about voluntary roles than in times gone by, surveys still indicate that more people would volunteer if it was easier to find out about opportunities.

The following chapters and the help list at the back of this book contain information about organisations that take volunteers, but first let's look at the differences between local and national organisations, ways of searching and applying for a voluntary opportunity, the sort of information likely to be requested and the questions you may want to ask organisations.

'Surveys still indicate that more people would volunteer if it was easier to find out about opportunities.'

Local versus national

Does it matter whether you volunteer for a small organisation closer to home, or a local branch of a large organisation? This is something only you can decide, but overleaf are some of the advantages and disadvantages to both which you might find useful:

Volunteering for a small, local organisation

Possible advantages:

- Working for a cause in your own community.
- Less administration.
- More hands-on experience.
- Less requirement to travel.
- More say over how funds raised are spent.

Possible disadvantages:

- Less money for training and publicity.
- Fewer opportunities to progress.
- Less support and management.

Volunteering for a national organisation

Possible advantages:

- More likely to have dedicated volunteer managers.
- Better training and supervision.
- More opportunities for progression.

Possible disadvantages:

- Feeling insignificant.
- More administration and red tape.
- Less connected with your community.

How do I find out more?

Word of mouth

Even in these days of mobile technology, one of the best ways of finding out about voluntary opportunities can be through word of mouth. Not only will you get the contact details of an organisation, but by speaking to someone who has volunteered with an organisation, you'll also get an idea of whether it is right for you.

Try asking around amongst your family, friends, colleagues or neighbours – it won't take long to find someone who has volunteered at some stage.

Volunteering as a result of an initial local contact can help you feel better connected to a cause. However, if someone you know has had a negative experience of volunteering with an organisation, don't rule it out automatically. If the organisation appears to have the right role for you, it might still be worth contacting them direct and sharing your concerns, or making enquiries about them at your local volunteer bureau.

Via the Internet

Most volunteer-involving organisations today have their own website, and actively encourage contact via the Internet. Some of them have a general email address and others have a specific email contact for enquiries about volunteering with them.

Many of the larger organisations have an online enquiry form asking for your basic contact details and the type of voluntary opportunity you are interested in. In most cases, this information is then sent to your nearest local branch of the charity. Someone from this local branch will then make contact with you.

By phone

The quickest way to find a phone number for a charity is once again via the Internet. Some large organisations have national helplines from where you will be directed to someone who can speak to you about volunteering with them. Others don't have a national helpline but on their website you can search for the telephone number for your nearest local branch.

'Even in these days of mobile technology, one of the best ways of finding out about voluntary opportunities can be through word of mouth.'

If you are unable to access the Internet, the best way to obtain the phone number of an organisation you are interested in volunteering with is to get in touch with your local volunteer bureau or ask at your nearest library.

By post

Sending postal enquires to volunteer-involving organisations is actively discouraged these days – many charities do not have the staff at their central offices to deal with incoming post from prospective volunteers around the country.

As with telephoning, if you are unable to access the Internet, the best way to obtain the contact details of an organisation is to get in touch with your local volunteer bureau, or ask at your nearest library.

Using a volunteer-involving agency

If you don't have a specific charity in mind, it's a good idea to get advice from one of the excellent volunteer-involving or 'umbrella' organisations that now exist. Whether you use the Internet, or prefer to discuss things face-to-face, at least one of the following organisations will be able to advise you.

Volunteer centres

Volunteer England has a network of volunteer centres that spans the country. These are local organisations that provide support and expertise within the local community, to potential volunteers, existing volunteers and organisations that involve volunteers.

Volunteer centres are often a good place to start looking for volunteering opportunities in the local area. They can find out what you're interested in doing, and try to match you with a suitable volunteering role with a local charity or voluntary organisation.

'Sending postal enquires to volunteer-involving organisations is actively discouraged these days.'

Do-it

Do-it.org.uk is a national database of volunteering opportunities in the UK. Go to www.do-it.org.uk and enter your area of interest, the type of activity you wish to do and where you live. You will then be offered a list of possible volunteering opportunities in your area.

TimeBank

TimeBank is a national charity that provides people with the inspiration, opportunities and support to volunteer. It was created for those who know their time and skills are in demand, but do not know where to begin.

TimeBank constantly develops new, exciting ways to involve volunteers and its projects address very real needs. People who register with TimeBank have access to an online chat forum where they can get all their volunteering questions answered.

Go to www.timebank.org.uk and enter your postcode to find out about volunteering opportunities near you.

Using your local council

You can also find out about local voluntary opportunities through your local council. All councils these days have a website, some of which display information about local volunteering and vacancies. Councils are all contactable by phone or post.

Local libraries and community centres

If you don't have access to the Internet, or prefer to make enquiries face-to-face, your local library or community centre will be able to signpost you to the best organisation to help with your volunteering query.

Summing Up

- Once you've thought about why you want to volunteer, found a cause that motivates you, and have an idea of the sort of role that will suit you, it's time make contact and get involved.

- Does it matter whether you volunteer for a small organisation closer to home, or a local branch of a large organisation?

- Even in these days of mobile technology, one of the best ways of finding out about voluntary opportunities can be through word of mouth.

- Most volunteer-involving organisations today have their own website, and actively encourage contact via the Internet.

- If you don't have a specific charity in mind, it's a good idea to get advice from one of the excellent 'umbrella' organisations that now exist.

Chapter Six

Making your Application

Make sure you have the information and notes from previous chapters in this book handy when you contact an organisation. This will make the process much quicker and easier for you.

Organisations working with volunteers will all have slightly different ways of taking on volunteers. Some organisations will have recruitment information on their website and others will ask you to fill out an application form or go for an informal interview.

This is not like applying for a job. The organisation will just want to find out whether you have the basic skills they need and whether they can offer you the kind of opportunity you want.

Volunteering opportunities can be short term or long term, part-time or full-time. The application process for a one-day volunteering opportunity, for example, to weed a garden, will be very different to an ongoing more formal role, for example being a Scout leader.

If the role has some responsibility, for example handling money, or if you will be working with vulnerable people or with dangerous equipment, you may be asked to go to an interview. This will give you and the organisation a chance to assess each other and ask questions.

'This is not like applying for a job.'

Questions you may be asked

* Why are you interested in volunteering?
* What sort of volunteering activities are you interested in?
* What skills would you bring to the volunteering role?
* Are there any new skills you would like to learn through volunteering?

- How much time do you have to offer, and when are you available?
- Do you have a driving licence?
- Can you attend an informal local interview/chat?
- Can you supply references?

Questions you might want to ask

What is the aim of the organisation?

Most organisations will have a statement of intent or belief. Make sure you support what the organisation stands for and believes in.

What does the position involve?

'Make sure you support what the organisation stands for and believes in.'

Having a clear understanding of what you will be doing is vital. It helps you decide if the work is what you really had in mind when you first thought about giving your time. Are you physically and emotionally suited to the opportunity? Is there any chance you could lose interest within a few weeks?

Where will I be based?

There's no point working in a place you don't like. Be honest. If you've always wanted to work outdoors then make sure you aren't stuck behind a desk.

Equally, if you want to work in the community, listening and caring for people, make sure you don't end up spending hours on committees or answering emails at home.

Will I be out of pocket?

Most organisations cover reasonable out-of-pocket expenses, but never assume this to be the case, so always ask.

Are there any qualifications I can gain?

Make it clear at the outset if you are interested in gaining a qualification – this way the training could be tailored to suit your goal.

Some organisations may offer qualifications such as NVQs. If you do need a formal qualification, it may be best to contact your local volunteer centre as they may know of local organisations that offer qualifications.

What if it doesn't work out?

You are under no formal obligation to keep volunteering for an organisation if your circumstances change and/or you want to leave. However, it is always worth talking to someone at the organisation about this first. You can discuss with them why you feel unhappy and what you feel would improve your time as a volunteer in the organisation.

If you feel that something is seriously wrong or someone is treating you badly you should consider making a complaint to the organisation.

Am I allowed to volunteer?

Any good organisation should apply the same rules on diversity as they do for paid staff. All organisations are encouraged to have an equal opportunities policy in place, which you should ask to see if you feel you have been unfairly treated.

People with disabilities

People with a disability can volunteer, but transport arrangements have been found to be one of the biggest barriers to volunteering for people with physical disabilities.

If you think your disability might make it difficult for you to volunteer, call up and have a chat with the volunteering team at the relevant organisation about your needs. They will be able to advise you on which of their voluntary opportunities are accessible, and also make sure that their staff members do their best to ensure you can volunteer the way you want to.

If your disability is not physical, it is up to you whether you disclose it. If you do, the organisation may be better placed to offer support, such as arranging for you to take more breaks.

'Some organisations may offer qualifications such as NVQs.'

People claiming state benefits

Volunteering will not affect your benefits, and you can volunteer for as many hours as you like. You should, however, tell your benefits advisor that you are volunteering.

Asylum seekers/refugees

People who have refugee status or have exceptional leave to remain are allowed to do any type of work, including voluntary work. You may have a letter saying that you must not engage in paid work – but this does not apply to roles that are voluntary and you are entitled to receive out-of-pocket expenses.

However, if you want to volunteer with children or vulnerable adults and are a recent arrival to the UK, your Criminal Records Bureau (CRB) check might take some time.

Children and young people

If you are under 18, then there is no legal reason why you cannot volunteer. You will find that some organisations may not be willing to take you on – particularly if their volunteer roles are not supervised all the time or may involve risk.

Your parent or guardian will be asked to give permission for you to volunteer.

Many people under 18 do volunteer, and there are plenty of roles that are safe and suitable for them.

People with a criminal record

Many people with past convictions worry that they will not be able to volunteer. This is not true at all. Under the Rehabilitation of Offenders Act, only organisations that work with children and/or vulnerable adults are allowed to ask about spent convictions.

Organisations are only entitled to apply for a CRB Disclosure if a person will be volunteering in a 'regulated activity' as detailed by the CRB. For more information go to www.crb.homeoffice.gov.uk and click on, 'faqs', then, 'definitions'.

Some organisations might ask about any unspent convictions, but this should only be in relation to the volunteering role that you are applying for. Anything you tell an organisation about past convictions should remain confidential.

What you should expect as a volunteer

An induction

For most part-time ongoing volunteering roles within an organisation you should expect an induction, where you are told about the organisation and its policies. This would generally cover health and safety, what to do if you have a problem and an introduction to other staff and volunteers.

A named supervisor

You should be told who your supervisor or leader is and how to contact them. It is important that you have a named person who you can go to with any problems or queries.

Adequate training

Some organisations offer a lot of training and support, but others don't and expect you to learn 'on the job' or contribute your existing skills. You will need to ask the organisation you are intending to volunteer with.

It also depends on the tasks that you will be doing. For example, if you are spending one day clearing overgrowth from paths, you can expect about 15 minutes training where you are told:

- What to do.
- How to use the tools.
- What health and safety precautions to take.

On the other hand, if you volunteer to give welfare benefits advice you should get much more training, including:

- Training sessions spread over several weeks.
- Ongoing training to keep you up to date.

'Some organisations offer a lot of training and support, but others don't and expect you to learn 'on the job' or contribute your existing skills.'

Setting boundaries

Feeling strongly about a particular cause, does not mean you are willing, or able, to slot into several roles in order to support it. If you are short of time or energy, this is something you need to be clear about from the outset in order to avoid future misunderstandings. Remember – this is your time you are donating so you should enjoy what you do as a volunteer!

Case study – Setting boundaries

'I was diagnosed with a long-term health condition and had to retire early. I'm a fairly quiet person and don't have a lot of energy, but while I could, I wanted to play a small part in helping others affected by the same condition.

'I volunteered for the local support group and was asked to help with a tin shake at our local supermarket, which was fine as a one-off, but afterwards it seemed expected of me to get involved in all sorts of exhausting events.

'I didn't have the confidence to refuse. I'd hoped to just do an occasional, behind the scenes role like counting money or stuffing envelopes – but it felt like you had to be involved in everything or nothing at all. In the end I resigned because it was making me feel ill.' Jane, 45.

Summing Up

- Make sure you have the information and notes from previous chapters in this book handy when you contact an organisation.

- This is not like applying for a job. The organisation will just want to find out whether you have the basic skills they need and whether they can offer you the kind of opportunity you want.

- Be prepared to answer questions about your reasons for wanting to volunteer with a particular organisation and any relevant skills or experience.

- Do not be afraid to ask your own questions of the organisation – it is better for you and for them to resolve any queries from the outset.

- As a volunteer, you can expect to be treated fairly at all times and have an induction, a named supervisor, adequate training and out-of-pocket expenses.

- Feeling strongly about a particular cause, does not mean you are willing, or able, to slot into several roles in order to support it

- Remember – this is your time you are donating so you should enjoy what you do as a volunteer!

Chapter Seven

What Else do I
Need to Know?

The following chapters contain personal case studies from volunteers in a variety of organisations along with a directory of such organisations. Before we move on, this chapter covers some of the necessary legal issues.

Although most legal obligations rest with the organisation you are volunteering for, it is important that you understand the legal and organisational issues in the voluntary sector.

Contracts

It is important to understand that as a volunteer, you are not afforded the same legal protection as paid employees.

Apart from actual expenses, the only other benefits you receive as a volunteer should be in training to improve your skills and, if relevant, accommodation or pocket money.

Insurance

All organisations that take volunteers on should have an insurance policy to cover them, either under employer's liability insurance or public liability insurance.

If you are working with vulnerable people or if you are using specialist equipment, it is important that the organisation's insurance covers you. Check that you will be fully insured under its policy.

'It is important to understand that as a volunteer, you are not afforded the same legal protection as paid employees.'

Volunteer drivers

If part of your volunteering work is to transport people around in your own vehicle, you will need to inform your insurers that you will be using it for voluntary work. Make sure you specifically say you are using your vehicle for voluntary and not commercial work, and that you will only be receiving expenses.

In theory, this should not increase your premium, but if it does, it may be worth shopping around for a better offer. The organisation you are volunteering for should reimburse you for any extra expenses that being a voluntary worker brings.

Health and safety

Organisations have a duty of care towards volunteers, so steps should be taken to reduce the probability of an injury, perhaps through training, the use of appropriate safety clothing and supervision.

If you are not told when you begin volunteering, then find out what the procedures are should you, or someone you are caring for or working with, need medical attention. Who is the person in charge of first aid? Or in case of fire, whose responsibility is it to ensure everyone is out of the building?

Equal opportunities

All organisations are obliged by law not to discriminate against workers because of gender, marital status, disability, colour, race, nationality or ethnic origin. This legal requirement relates to paid workers, so as a volunteer you will not automatically have the same rights. However, all good organisations will have an equal opportunities policy in place, which they should apply to both paid and voluntary workers.

Fundraising

Rules about fundraising

There are quite a few legal issues related to raising money for charity. The most important ones are:

- You can only raise money for a registered charity.
- All the money you raise must go straight to the registered charity.
- The charity's registered number must be on all fundraising materials.
- To collect money on the street you must be over 16 and sealed buckets must be used.
- All fundraising must be supervised by someone over 18.
- All monies collected must be managed by someone over 18.

Hiring an external venue for an event

If you hire an external venue for your event, check that they have all the correct licences. A reputable venue will be able to show you the licence, their public liability insurance policy and the health and safety policy.

It is also useful to talk to the relevant local authority if you want to organise an outdoor event as applications need to be made three months in advance, but each local authority will work slightly differently.

Sponsorship and donations

All requests for donations to charity must have an attached registered charity number. All funds raised by you for the charity must only be received by this charity organisation.

Any personal data collected about donors or supporters must only be used in compliance with the Data Protection Act 1998. When a proportion of the money raised is being used to cover all or some costs, this must be made clear to donors.

'All requests for donations to charity must have an attached registered charity number.'

Collections

There are various licences you might need if you are going to make a collection. For all collections made in public places you must have a street collection licence, which can be obtained from the relevant local authority.

During all collections, you must wear ID badges and use sealed collection tins.

Raffles and lotteries

If you want to hold a raffle at a one-off event, you must sell tickets solely at the event.

If you do not spend over £250 on prizes (donated goods do not count) and do not give money prizes (vouchers do not count) it will count as a small lottery, for which you do not need a licence.

'There are
various licences
you might
need if you are
going to make
a collection.'

The result of the raffle must also be drawn at the event. If your lottery or raffle does not fit into this description then you will need a lotteries licence from your local council or metropolitan borough. Liability for the legal organisation of a lottery falls onto the person/persons promoting it.

Summing Up

- Although most legal obligations rest with the organisation you are volunteering for, it is important that you understand the legal and organisational issues in the voluntary sector.

- It is important to understand that as a volunteer, you are not afforded the same legal protection as paid employees.

- All organisations that take volunteers on should have an insurance policy to cover them, either under employer's liability insurance or public liability insurance.

- If part of your volunteering work is to transport people around in your own vehicle, you will need to inform your insurers that you will be using it for voluntary work.

- Organisations have a duty of care towards volunteers, so steps should be taken to reduce the probability of an injury, perhaps through training, the use of appropriate safety clothing and supervision.

- All good organisations will have an equal opportunities policy in place, which they should apply to both paid and voluntary workers.

- There are quite a few legal issues related to raising money for charity. The organisation you are volunteering for should provide you with the necessary training in order for you to understand them and apply them.

Chapter Eight

Health and Social Care – Volunteer Experiences

This chapter provides case studies from a few of the many charities and organisations working in health and social care and which use volunteers in a huge variety of roles. Contact information for these organisations and others can be found in the help list at the end of this book.

Advice and counselling

Advice and counselling organisations play an important role in the community. A lot of people need support at some time in their life. If you have the patience and skills then, with the correct training, this might be the opportunity for you.

Delphi, 36
Volunteer with Cruse Bereavement Care

www.crusebereavementcare.org.uk

'My journey with Cruse started in September 2002, when I applied to attend the Cruse Bereavement Training (now called the Awareness in Bereavement Care course). I immediately felt a connection not just with the trainers but with the organisation as a whole.

'I hadn't done any volunteering before this, but I'd thought about volunteering and I knew that I wanted to do something in a supporting role, so when I saw the advert for Cruse Training I sent away for more details straight away.

> ' I immediately felt a connection not just with the trainers but with the organisation as a whole.'
>
> Delphi, 36

'I took a break from volunteering in 2009 but I've been with Cruse in total for about eight years. My roles have varied and have included Bereavement Support Volunteer, Telephone Referral Secretary, Area Management Committee Member and Area Trainer. My most recent, new role is as Area Fundraiser and I've just established the Fundraising Committee so we can start organising some local events.

'I would say the most useful skills for my roles with Cruse have come from time spent actually doing it. The training and supervision from within the organisation combined with the skills, experience and valuable input from other colleagues has been absolutely essential not just to my personal development, but in understanding the nature of the work and how it can be most effective.

'The clients teach me every day. My mentor always said the day you stop being touched by a client's story, was the day you should hang up your supporting gloves – which she did the day she died in 2009. It showed me that you can still feel compassion for a person without being disabled by their grief – I can be human and helpful at the same time.

'Although life experiences and relationships teach us something about who we think we are, this doesn't mean we know everything about other people. One of the biggest parts of the learning journey for a new trainee is realising that even though they may have been bereaved this doesn't mean they know how to help everyone – at least, not on the strength of that alone.

'One person's experience of bereavement is different to another (even when two people mourn the same person) and that's why the training is so invaluable. That said, if you have an honest intention to help someone and you can sit comfortably with them whilst they tell you their story without feeling the need to 'fix' them, you will have the makings of a great volunteer with Cruse.'

Jackie, 65
Volunteer with Relate

www.relate.org.uk

'I began volunteering as a marriage guidance counsellor about 30 years ago after an old friend asked if I'd help him run some local sessions. Before that I'd been involved with the Brownies and Guides. In my 'day job' I worked as an accountant.

'After moving to a different part of the country, I wanted to meet people and get involved in the local community. I started as a volunteer receptionist for Relate, before becoming a trustee on their board of directors and then training for my present role as a counsellor. My employers were very supportive, allowing me time for annual training days with Relate and some flexibility with my paid hours.

'I'm a widow now and retired from my paid job, but just as committed to my voluntary role and still work 8-9 hours per week there – I believe you have to be as committed as colleagues employed in a paid role with the same charity. Most people I meet through my role don't know I'm a volunteer – I don't do it for recognition. I've made many great friends through volunteering and it has enabled me to feel connected with my community. I would recommend it.'

Children and families

Organisations that work with children, young people and families often need volunteers to run clubs, supervise activities, or help with mentoring schemes. Voluntary experience can give you a valuable insight into work with children and young people, as well as being enjoyable and rewarding in itself.

'I've made many great friends through volunteering and it has enabled me to feel connected with my community. I would recommend it.'
Jackie, 65

Sue
Volunteer with Home-Start

www.home-start.org.uk

Sue had resigned herself to the fact that her son did not want children, which meant that she would never be a grandparent. 'I just accepted it,' she said. 'I adore children though and dreamed of having lots of grandchildren, but life doesn't always give you what you want.'

All that changed though when a Home-Start leaflet dropped through Sue's door. She decided to sign up for the training course and before she knew it she was busy supporting families with young children.

'The support that Home-Start offers its volunteers after the training course is brilliant,' says Sue, 'and the ongoing training means that there is always something new to learn. It also helps in my personal life. I lost confidence after I had to give up work because of ill health and although I now have a certain amount of control on my condition, without Home-Start I would never have got my confidence back.'

Sue is able to offer both practical and emotional support to her families and really enjoys the time that she spends on home visits. she says: 'I sometimes get mothers with low self-esteem and depression who don't know how to play with their children, so I take on a grandmother's role. I read them stories, run around the garden and play mad games with them. I care about them the same way I would have done my own.'

Stephanie
Volunteer with Action for Children

www.actionforchildren.org.uk

'I was attracted to working in a children's centre to gain a well-rounded experience so that I can deliver the best quality provision when I qualify – I'm studying for Early Years Professional Status.

'I enjoy working with the children as well as their families. I am really enjoying the opportunities for development available to me at the children's centre. The staff encourage me to experience as much as possible and let me develop as much as I feel that I am ready for.

'I am learning every day. I am taking on more new responsibilities than when I worked in a private nursery. The opportunities for involvement with many different people and families are frequent. Many different schemes mean that I am exposed to new experiences.

'I feel that I am having a positive impact on the team. I believe that I am now fully integrated and can be relied upon.'

Beth
Volunteer with Action for Children

www.actionforchildren.org.uk

'I volunteer at a Children's Centre, helping new mothers as part of the breastfeeding support group. I enjoy being part of the breastfeeding support group because I am so passionate about breastfeeding. It really appealed to me to be able to help others.

'I enjoy coming every week and giving my time to this service and it is especially nice to give something back. It's very sociable, great to meet lots of new people and also fun being part of a group that regularly meets and seeing supportive and different faces every week.

'It is a very supportive group with lots of different parenting styles, advice and ideas. There are new ways of doing things that I wouldn't have thought of myself. I have got lots of experience with breastfeeding my three children. I have had many trials and challenges myself that I can pass on to others. I do lots of research and keep up to date with the latest studies so I can pass these ideas on.'

'I enjoy coming every week and giving my time to this service and it is especially nice to give something back.'

Beth

Nicola
Volunteer with Action for Children

www.actionforchildren.org.uk

'I volunteer because it's my community and I want to give something back by supporting families to overcome barriers in their lives. I've learnt to always ask questions and never assume the answer. Getting my recent OCN Level 2 qualification in 'Supporting Families' was a huge achievement. Every moment with such a supportive team of volunteers has been memorable.'

Kirsty
Volunteer with Action for Children

www.actionforchildren.org.uk

'I volunteer because I'm interested in helping people and sharing my own experiences as a parent. My work involves supporting groups of parents to build their parenting skills. I've learnt to be open and honest and ask for support when I need it.

'Volunteering has helped me to feel so much more confident in all areas of my life.

'Being part of a community play and acting out issues that my community faces was brilliant.'

Health and disability

There are many health charities working to better the lives of people from all sections of the community who are coping with illness, disabilities or emotional difficulties. The volunteering opportunities in this field are wide and varied.

While some training may be needed, a sense of compassion and patience is vital if you want to get involved.

Claire
Volunteer with the British Heart Foundation

www.bhf.org.uk/volunteer

Claire, who suffers from spina bifida, has volunteered at her local BHF shop since 2008, going in for two half days each week.

In 2011 she successfully completed a Retail Diploma Qualification (NVQ level 2). Claire was chosen as 'Learner of the Year', from 5,500 learners who completed the same qualification across national mainstream retailers and charities. She was nominated for the award by her assessor, who highlighted Claire's commitment both to the BHF and to getting the award.

Claire adds, 'I hope that my success will inspire others to volunteer and get a qualification.'

David* (*Name changed)
Volunteer with the Red Cross

www.redcross.org.uk

Over the past three years, David's* alcohol problem has cost him his marriage, his job and very nearly his life. But now, helped by a Red Cross volunteer, he's putting his life back together. The father-of-one was diagnosed with liver failure in 2007 and given two weeks to live. He recovered but then went on a downward spiral of regular binges and now lives with his mother.

David* finally turned a corner after being referred to the Red Cross' supported discharge service – part of the Red Cross' care in the home service – which helps people with drug and alcohol problems after they leave hospital. Helped by caseworker Helen, he has signed up to a 12-week residential rehab course.

He said, 'If it wasn't for Helen, I wouldn't have accessed any benefits or known how to contact the drug and alcohol social workers. She's never given up. Helen's belief in me instils me with a bit more belief in myself. Her impartiality is important too, because it makes me less wary of speaking out.' David's mother added, 'It's been a lot better since Helen started helping us. If I want to phone, she's always there. Until she got involved, we'd been up against a brick wall.'

'I hope that my success will inspire others to volunteer and get a qualification.'

Claire

Louise, 45
Volunteer with the Multiple Sclerosis Society

www.mssociety.org.uk

'I was just 38 when I was first diagnosed with MS. It was a huge shock. On top of my MS symptoms I became depressed and increasingly isolated. Volunteering for my local branch of the MS Society has given me a new sense of purpose.

'I've met many people through the branch – some have become close friends. We are there for each other when our MS symptoms or medications get us down and also to celebrate when things are going well.

'I help run a monthly drop-in for people who are newly diagnosed with MS. I try and share what I have learnt about my condition in a positive way, so that they might not struggle as much as I did in the early days.

'With a long-term health condition, there is nothing as helpful as being able to chat informally with others who understand exactly what you are talking about. I try and support others by listening and signposting them to helpful organisations.'

'Volunteering
for my local
branch of the
MS Society
has given me
a new sense
of purpose.'
Louise, 45

Elderly health and care

Organisations that provide help to older people usually need volunteers to work at lunch clubs, help in care homes, or transport those who are unable to drive to and from a function or to the hospital or doctor's surgery for medical care. Some simply need volunteers to spend time with an older person who perhaps has no close friends or family, or who is unable to leave their home, very often due to illness.

Kathy, 60
Volunteer with the WRVS

www.wrvs.org.uk

'I had been thinking for some time about doing some voluntary work when I stopped work, so when I saw a notice in the library for volunteers to take books to housebound people, I signed up. I've always loved reading and libraries, and thought it would be good to help others enjoy both those things. The scheme is run by the WRVS and co-ordinated by the library. The WRVS takes care of all the formalities, including a CRB check, and reimburses necessary expenses – mostly parking and mileage.

'The library tries to match volunteers geographically with people wanting to use the service. I only visit two people so far, but my round could grow. Just once a month I go to the library to select books, tapes or whatever against a list of preferences, take them to the users and then return the books no longer needed. I stay and chat for about half an hour at each home, and really enjoy those conversations.'

Housing, Welfare and Addiction

Heidi, 23
Volunteer with BTCV

www2.btcv.org.uk

Heidi, 23, volunteers at a homeless shelter for rough sleepers and the previously homeless in London, through the UK volunteering charity, CSV. Heidi wants to gain hands-on experience and pursue her passion for volunteering after graduating from the University of Durham with a degree in Anthropology.

She is adamant that volunteering for CSV has given her the perfect opportunity to explore her desire to work in the charity sector. Heidi says, 'Throughout university, I knew I wanted to work in the third sector, but I had little experience in homelessness or working for charities in the UK. CSV has given me excellent hands-on experience.'

The job involves a routine of serving food in the canteen, providing hot drinks, ensuring towels are clean and dry each day for the rough sleepers to have showers and giving out clothing donations. It also involves working closely with external agencies such as counsellors, the NHS and mental health organisations.

Heidi says, 'Although some of these tasks may sound like small aids, they are a vital lifeline for the people that come into the centre every day, giving them structure and helping them to keep their dignity whilst on the streets.'

She is now working full-time for a London-based homeless charity as a trainee key-worker which she believes is as a result of her experience with CSV. Heidi encourages other people to volunteer, 'I really did have the best year of my life, with some lovely people who took a lot of time investing in the volunteers, and making the experience valuable and transferable. As well as having a lot of fun.'

Criminal Justice System

This type of voluntary work is demanding and requires specific skills, abilities, checks and training, but will almost certainly challenge some of your pre-conceptions about victims of crime, young offenders, prisoners, prisoners' families, prisons, and the people who work in them.

David, 40
Volunteer with the Youth Offending Service

'My foster parents were a real inspiration to me. They gave up so much of their time as well as their home. Now I'm a parent myself with a settled home life, I wanted to give something back so I volunteer part-time as an Appropriate Adult with my local youth offending service.

'My role is to support young people whilst they are in custody if they don't have a parent or guardian who can attend. Some of them are really frightened. Others are regular visitors at the police station and appear to take it all in their stride. But you can tell that deep down they are scared and need someone to be there for them in a non-judgmental way.

'I check that they understand what is happening whilst they are in custody and that they have been treated okay and have been offered food and drink. I also ask them if they have a solicitor and about any medical or accommodation issues, then alert the relevant people as necessary.

'I don't ask them about the circumstances of their arrest, but I sit in with them when they are interviewed by the police. They always seem surprised that I am more interested in them than what they have done – and amazed to learn that I'm a volunteer and not being paid!

'When I come away from the police station it makes me so grateful for my own life and puts things in perspective. I hope I've shown these young people that society does care about them and wants to help them break out of crime.'

Louise, 29
Volunteer with Victim Support

www.victimsupport.org.uk

'I joined Victim Support whilst I was at home after my first baby and had some spare time at evenings and weekends when my partner was home to look after her. My late younger brother had been convicted after a serious assault and I often wondered about the victims of his crime. This was my way of giving back in some small way, for the way my life had turned out compared to my brother's, and to try and help with the damage caused to the lives of victims.

'My role was to visit victims of crime in their homes following notification from my co-ordinator – if they had indicated to the police that they would find a visit from Victim Support helpful. I listened to them, helped them fill in paperwork and signposted them to other useful organisations if necessary.

'I made it clear from the start that I could only volunteer for a few hours each week and this wasn't a problem. It was a real eye-opener for me, realising that these crimes were going on in my own neighbourhood, and seeing the devastating effects on the victims. But it gave me a sense of purpose outside my own safe world and helped me to feel connected with my community.'

'It was a real eye-opener for me, realising that these crimes were going on in my own neighbourhood, and seeing the devastating effects on the victims.'

Louise, 29

Summing Up

- There are many charities and organisations working in health and social care and which use volunteers in a huge variety of roles.

- Advice and counselling organisations play an important role in the community. A lot of people need support at some time in their life.

- Organisations that work with children, young people and families often need volunteers to run clubs, supervise activities, or help with mentoring schemes.

- There is a wide variety of health charities working to better the lives of people from all sections of the community who are coping with illness, disabilities or emotional difficulties.

- Organisations that provide help to older people usually need volunteers to work at lunch clubs, help in care homes, or transport those who are unable to drive. Sometimes volunteers are simply needed to spend time with an older person.

- Volunteering in the Criminal Justice System can be demanding and requires specific skills, abilities, checks and training, but will almost certainly challenge some of your pre-conceptions.

Chapter Nine

Other Volunteer Experiences

As stressed throughout this book, there are now far more ways to volunteer than ever before. This chapter provides case studies from many more vital charities and organisations across the UK which offer new and exciting ways to volunteer.

Animals and animal welfare

There are many ways to work with animals, not all of them mean you have to work directly with them. You can also volunteer for non-animal jobs like events organising or photography for an animal or wildlife charity.

Clare
Volunteer with Hearing Dogs for Deaf People

www.hearingdogs.org.uk

'In my view, there are very few things as fulfilling as volunteering for Hearing Dogs for Deaf People as you know your work will ultimately lend itself towards helping the life of a deaf person.

'My particular volunteer role is hugely enjoyable. You get to experience all the normal joys involved with having a pet dog, but once a year you also witness the wonderful birth of a litter of puppies. It really is such a brilliant experience and one of the unique volunteer roles within any charity.'

'In my view, there are very few things as fulfilling as volunteering for Hearing Dogs for Deaf People.'

Clare

Kate, 64
Volunteer with The Blue Cross (Pet Bereavement Support Service)

www.bluecross.org.uk

'I wanted to join this admirable service after losing a dog myself and realising that support is so badly needed. I had helped many people to cope after losing a pet but realised that it was also necessary to have some training to enable me to offer the most appropriate help and support. By joining the Pet Bereavement Support Service as a volunteer I was able to channel my learning and experience and be involved in a well-respected animal charity.

'I'm involved in a number of ways with the service. Sometimes I work a few sessions as a "duty volunteer" where I'm the first point of contact on a national support line and answer calls from home. We offer emotional support and practical information for anyone experiencing the loss of a pet, whatever the circumstances. I take brief details from the caller, help to put them at their ease, and pass their call through to a volunteer who offers the support.

'In my other role as a "support volunteer" I offer emotional support and comfort but above all, listen and allow the caller to talk about their loss. We all volunteer from home and work through a "virtual call centre". This approach helps us to keep our contact details confidential and it also means that wherever you are in the country you can volunteer on the support line without having to travel anywhere! I also act as a 'buddy' and friendly support for new volunteers joining.

'I really enjoy my role as a support line volunteer with The Blue Cross as it gives me a real sense of purpose, of being able to make a difference to a caller's day. It also allows me to give something back to society.'

Ray
Volunteer Educational Speaker with The Blue Cross

www.bluecross.org.uk

When I took early retirement I knew that I would need to find some new activities. I decided I would seek some charity work which would enable me to make a difference to others.

It was at one of our visits to Crufts that I visited the Blue Cross stand and took away some information about the organisation. Whilst reading the brochures I saw an opportunity which really appealed to me; I could become a volunteer speaker! This would enable me to work with my dog, Barney, whilst helping to educate children at key stages in their development. I realised that it was also a learning opportunity for me.

I applied and, after an interview and CRB check, I completed a two stage home study course covering the history and work of the Blue Cross, care of animals, choosing a pet and preparing talks for various age groups. Barney also had a stringent test to ensure that he was suited to working in the education environment. Thankfully we were both successful and, after getting our identity badges and kit, we were ready for our first talk to a Brownie pack.

I was pleasantly surprised at how well the subject of 'safety around animals' was received and how much the pack enjoyed the interactivity with Barney. This talk was followed by other requests and, in less than a year, Barney and I have visited over 800 children focusing mainly on safety around animals and the work of The Blue Cross.

This work provides a very educational and enjoyable pastime which also promotes the good work of the charity and helps people to be more aware of animals and their welfare. I continue to learn and am rewarded by the recommendations for further talks, contributions to the charity and hearing the children telling their parents 'you should ask before you touch a dog' when they approach Barney after the meeting!

'When I took early retirement I knew that I would need to find some new activities.'

Ray

Arts, Environment and Heritage

Volunteering in the arts, environment or heritage can enable you to make a positive difference in your community.

Richard
Volunteer with Create Arts

www.createarts.org.uk www.voluntaryarts.org.uk

'I volunteered for Create because I love the arts, and the charity uses the creative arts in such a special way, helping people who are vulnerable or disadvantaged. This particular event, creative:space, is a perfect example, giving disabled children and their families the opportunity to attend an interactive concert together.

'On the day, there were two events. We volunteers were assigned a range of duties, from setting up tables and blowing up balloons to welcoming the families, helping them to settle in and encouraging them to participate as they felt comfortable. It was a very hands-on experience and I appreciated being asked to complete a questionnaire at the end. Create really wanted to find out what I thought and how I had found the experience.

'I was very impressed with the level of commitment and organisation that the Create team brought to the event. The attention to detail was incredible – nothing had been left to chance. They all got involved and their passion for what they were doing was infectious! I really enjoyed working with the families – helping children to decorate hand puppets; handing out percussion instruments; and even dancing!

'It was inspiring seeing the joy on the faces of children and adults alike and several families told me that this is a rare opportunity. There are few places where they can go where they feel fully accepted. The smiling faces of the children as they involved themselves in the dancing and the music was probably my favourite part.

'I volunteered for Create because I love the arts.'

Richard

'Volunteering for creative:space reminded me how comfortable and healthy my own life is. I found it grounding to offer my time to families who are not always able to enjoy what I do. It only takes such a small amount of time to give something so valuable to a charity that's doing truly wonderful work. I would recommend it 100%.'

Rob
Volunteer with BTCV

www2.btcv.org.uk

In a matter of weeks, Rob Griffin went from organising posh parties at footballers' mansions to being homeless and living in hostels.

'My life was glamorous; I travelled to places like Japan and Australia, but when I lost my job in the entertainment industry because of the recession, I hit rock bottom,' says Rob, 39. 'I was drinking too much and lost my house, ending up on the streets. I felt useless. In fact, I stopped feeling. I was at my lowest point.'

Homeless for four months, Rob eventually managed to get a flat. But he didn't know what to do with his days. 'I used to stay at home watching TV or go to the library,' he says. 'I was depressed.' That was before Rob started volunteering at BTCV's Hollybush Conservation Centre in Leeds five days a week. It's turned his life around. He's transformed an area used as a junkyard into a vegetable patch. He also co-ordinates other volunteers' work.

Rob's learned about plants as well as how to lead a group of people. He's now looking for work in horticulture. 'BTCV helped me totally change my outlook,' says Rob. 'I'm doing something worthwhile. I'm achieving and I've got people's respect. I'm not at the bottom of the pile anymore. I'm in control of my drinking and I'm really focused on where I want to be and how I'm going to get there.'

George, 15
Volunteer with the National Trust

www.nationaltrust.org.uk

'After doing some voluntary work in my local library over the summer holidays, I decided to look around for longer term opportunities and found an Oral History role at Tyntesfield. It sounded like a great opportunity as it involves both history and media which I have a passion for.

'Nine months down the line, my experience continues to amaze me. I am in a team of 15 creating the Tyntesfield Stories archives, finding people with memories of the estate and interviewing them to capture and preserve their memories; and sharing them with the community, whether that's with visitors to exhibitions or online to schools and museums. I also help out with other shorter projects such as the Easter trails to outdoor theatre days. That way I work with all sorts of people in the community; from people for whom Tyntesfield is a large part of their life to those who are only just discovering it.

'In my time at Tyntesfield I've been trained in the latest media technology, how to interview and what it means to be a volunteer with the National Trust. It's been a great experience – I've developed people skills, built up my confidence and enjoyed working with a team of volunteers and staff who are all really friendly and enthusiastic. I have some priceless skills and experiences to go on my CV, but it's also been a great way to spend my weekends and have fun. It's taught me how being a volunteer with the National Trust isn't just about being a room guide, but how diverse it really is and what a difference it can make in the community.'

> 'It's been a great experience – I've developed people skills, built up my confidence and enjoyed working with a team.'
>
> George, 15

Children and young people

Working with children and young people can be challenging but immensely rewarding. You'll never know how great an influence you can be until you try it.

Tom
Volunteer with The Prince's Trust

www.princes-trust.org.uk

Tom has been a volunteer with the Trust for the past three years. He originally volunteered as a business mentor, providing advice and support to young people starting their own businesses in Suffolk and Norfolk.

He chose to support The Prince's Trust as he felt he could use his own skills and experience to give something back to society and help young people to develop themselves and their lives.

After hearing about the new Enterprise Programme, Tom was keen to get involved as he felt it provided a magnificent opportunity for young people to develop life skills and he wishes such opportunities were available in his youth. Tom now supports day four of the Explore Enterprise course in Norfolk, helping young people to work on their interview skills and understand the value mentoring can add to their experiences with The Trust.

Tom says the best thing about volunteering with The Trust is being able to hear about the lives and hopes of young people, and being able to "give young people the chance to remake their lives and prove themselves".

Hilary
Volunteer with The Prince's Trust

www.princes-trust.org.uk

'When I was asked to volunteer, a combination of knowing that I had the practical experience needed to support these young people and the opportunity to challenge myself made the opportunity worth exploring. However it was only once I realised just how many volunteers were needed, along with the fact that there was a workshop conveniently close to home that I decided to sign up.

'Two other volunteers and I delivered a workshop to a terrific group of disadvantaged young people. The aim of the day was to help them find work placements as their first step to employment. The session was great, we talked through research and role-played the processes and skills required in finding a work placement.

'As volunteers we were certainly not surrogate teachers or lecturers, merely conduits to bring out the thoughts and answers that the young people themselves knew. A little gentle encouragement and positive feedback goes a very long way! We developed a fantastic sense of camaraderie, drawing strength from each other and improving our delivery.

'The young people were smashing, and incredibly well-behaved – even those who tried to hide it! A few were very shy so it was worth giving them some extra attention and a few extra minutes to build trust. I found meeting these young people incredibly inspiring, they opened my eyes to how little we really know about the lives going on around us.

'I really believe that I made a difference. My day was just one day out of a 12-week development programme. Hopefully instilling positive words, thoughts and action in these young people will stay with them. The team members were so enthusiastic, they want to learn, they want to grow, they just need someone to tell them they can and believe enough in them to give them a chance.

'I would definitely volunteer again and encourage everyone else to. The whole experience is a great leveller. Young people give out so much joy and humour. It's a pleasure to watch their confidence grow, even within one day. They're all winners, and by volunteering we are too!'

> **'I would definitely volunteer again and encourage everyone else to.'**
>
> Hilary

Sports

Without the two million adults who contribute at least one hour a week to volunteering in sport, community sport would grind to a halt. Volunteers also play an incredible role in staging some of England's most prestigious sporting events – including the 2012 Olympics.

Stuart, 47
Volunteer with Derbyshire County FA

'I played football at a good level from primary school onwards so it's part of who I am. After I injured my knee and had surgery, I realised with regret that my playing days were over. My son plays football too so I've been involved with his team and helped out as assistant manager, but realised that the day would come all too soon when he'd grow up and I'd really miss being involved with local football.

'I didn't want to manage a team – I tried it once before and it just wasn't for me. But I'd always wondered about being a referee, so I got in touch with my county FA and asked for some information.

'I decided to give it a try, did the training, and have been refereeing kids' football for three years now. It's been a steep learning curve, but I get a lot of satisfaction from it and it's great to be doing something active in the sport that I love.

Summing Up

- As stressed throughout this book, there are now far more ways to volunteer than ever before.

- There are many ways to work with animals, not all of them mean you have to work directly with them.

- Volunteering in the arts, environment or heritage can enable you to make a positive difference in your community.

- Working with children and young people can be challenging but immensely rewarding. You'll never know how great an influence you can be until you try it.

- Without the two million adults who contribute at least one hour a week to volunteering in sport, community sport would grind to a halt.

Help List

The volunteer-involving organisations listed here are just a small sample of the thousands working tirelessly in communities across the UK. For further information about other national and local organisations please contact your nearest volunteer centre, council or library or use one of the organisations listed at the end of this help list.

Advice and Counselling

Citizens Advice

Tel: 020 7833 2181 (administration only)
Helps people resolve their legal, money and other problems by providing free, independent and confidential advice, and by influencing policymakers.
Citizens Advice have a network of national and area field offices throughout England and Wales supporting the work of local Citizens Advice Bureau.
To locate your nearest CAB bureau go to www.citizensadvice.org.uk.

Cruse Bereavement Care

Websites: www.cruse.org.uk www.rd4u.org.uk (for children and young people)
Bereavement helpline: 0844 477 9400
Cruse Bereavement Care takes care of the life that's left, providing advice, information and support to anyone who has been bereaved (children, young people and adults), whenever or however the death occurred. The service is provided by trained, experienced volunteers and is confidential and free.
Cruse is the UK's leading bereavement care organisation with a network of 135 branches across England, Wales and Northern Ireland.

Relate

To locate your nearest Relate office, go to www.relate.org.uk
Tel: 0300 100 1234 (administration only)
Working to promote health, respect and justice in couples and family relationships. Services include relationship counselling for individuals and couples; family counselling; counselling for children and young people; and sex therapy. They also provide friendly and informal workshops for people at important life stages. Relate have a network of 77 centres throughout the UK.

Samaritans

www.samaritans.org
volunteering@samaritans.org
Volunteering Department, The Upper Mill, Kingston Road, Ewell, Surrey, KT17 2A
Tel: 08705 62 72 82 from the UK (volunteer recruitment helpline)
Samaritans is a confidential emotional support service for anyone in the UK and Ireland. The service is available 24 hours a day for people who are experiencing feelings of distress or despair, including those which may lead to suicide.

Children and Families

Action for Children

www.actionforchildren.org.uk
ask.us@actionforchildren.org.uk
Tel: 0300 123 2112
The leading UK provider of family and community centres, children's services in rural areas, services for disabled children and their families, and services for young people leaving care.

Barnado's

To locate your nearest office go to www.barnados.org.uk
info@barnardos.org.uk
Tel: 0208 550 8822 (head office)

Barnardo's works directly with children, young people and their families. It runs vital projects across the UK, including counselling for children who have been abused, fostering and adoption services, vocational training and disability inclusion groups.

Home-Start

To find your nearest scheme go to www.home-start.org.uk
Tel: 0800 068 63 68
Home-Start is a geographically diverse organisation made up of local Home-Starts and Home-Start UK. Home-Start supports vulnerable children and their families across the UK, helping them cope with postnatal illness, isolation, bereavement, disability, domestic violence and much more.

NSPCC

www.nspcc.org.uk
info@nspcc.org.uk
Tel: 020 7825 2775 (Information services)
The NSPCC protects children across the UK. They run a wide range of services for both children and adults, including national helplines and local projects.

Medical and Health

British Heart Foundation

Website: www.bhf.org.uk/volunteer
volunteer@bhf.org.uk
Tel: 0300 456 8353
The British Heart Foundation (BHF) is the nation's heart charity. 'Our vision is a world where people don't die prematurely from heart disease. We'll achieve this through pioneering research, vital prevention activity and ensuring quality care and support for everyone living with heart disease'.

British Red Cross

www.redcross.org.uk
information@redcross.org.uk
Tel: 0844 871 11 11

A volunteer-led humanitarian organisation that helps people in crisis, whoever and wherever they are, enabling vulnerable people at home and overseas to prepare for and respond to emergencies in their own communities.

Cancer Research

www.cancerresearchuk.org
volunteering@cancer.org.uk,
Tel:0845 009 4290
The world's leading charity dedicated to beating cancer through research.
'We've saved millions of lives with our groundbreaking work into preventing, diagnosing and treating cancer. People's chances of surviving cancer have doubled in the last 40 years, and we've been at the heart of that progress. But more than one in three of us will still get cancer at some point. Our vital work, funded entirely by the public, will help ensure that millions more people survive.'

Multiple Sclerosis Society

www.mssociety.org.uk
volunteering@mssociety.org.uk
Tel: 020 8438 0944 Volunteering Team
'The MS Society is the UK's largest charity for people affected by multiple sclerosis (MS). We are a membership organisation but provide services to all. The Society funds MS research, runs respite care centres, provides grants (financial assistance), education and training on MS. It produces numerous publications on MS and runs a freephone specialist helpline'.

St John Ambulance

www.sja.org.uk
Tel: 08700 10 49 50
St John Ambulance teaches people first aid – about 800,000 last year alone – so that they can be the difference between a life lost and a life saved.
'We teach young people in schools and through our activities for young people. We teach people in the workplace and provide first aid products. We teach people in the community. And we teach people who become our volunteers, who offer their skills and time to be the difference right in the

heart of their community – at public events, first responders or back-up to local ambulance services. As a charity, we're committed to making sure more people can be the difference between a life lost and a life saved'.

Disability

RNIB

http://www.rnib.org.uk
volunteering@rnib.org.uk
Tel: 0303 123 9999
'Royal National Institute of Blind People (RNIB) is the UK's leading charity offering information, support and advice to almost two million people with sight loss. Our pioneering work helps anyone with a sight problem – not just with braille and talking books, but with imaginative and practical solutions to everyday challenges. We also provide information on eye conditions and provide support and advice for people living with sight loss'.

RNID (Action Hearing Loss)

www.actiononhearingloss.org.uk
Tel: 0808 808 0123 (freephone)
Textphone: 0808 808 9000 (freephone)
'We aim to make a real difference to the lives of 10 million people who are deaf or have a hearing loss across the United Kingdom. You can help us. Our volunteers bring skills, experience, energy, enthusiasm and commitment to Action on Hearing Loss. And volunteering can make a difference in your life too, letting you meet new people and learn new skills'.

Scope

www.scope.org.uk
response@scope.org.uk
0808 800 3333
Scope is a charity that supports disabled people and their families.
'Our vision is a world where disabled people have the same opportunities to fulfill their life ambitions as non-disabled people'.

Housing and Homelessness

Crisis

www.crisis.org.uk
enquiries@crisis.org.uk
Tel: 0800 0 38 48 38
Crisis is the national charity for single homeless people.
'We are dedicated to ending homelessness by delivering life-changing services and campaigning for change. We could not change so many lives without the hard work and commitment of our volunteers. Over 10,000 people give their time, energy and skills to help deliver our services, campaign, fundraise and provide administrative and IT support'.

Shelter

www.shelter.org.uk
volunteering@shelter.org.uk
Tel: 0844 515 2182
'Shelter is a charity that works to alleviate the distress caused by homelessness and bad housing. We do this by giving advice, information and advocacy to people in housing need, and by campaigning for lasting political change to end the housing crisis for good. At Shelter we are always looking for volunteers. Apply to become one now to gain some valuable work experience – and the satisfaction of helping a good cause'.

Alcohol and Substance Misuse

Addiction Dependency Solutions (ADS)

www.adsolutions.org.uk
ADS@ADSolutions.org.uk
Tel: 0161 831 2400
ADS (Addiction Dependency Solutions) is the leading charity delivering drug and alcohol services across the north of England. We have over thirty service centres across the region working with in excess of 15,000 people last year.

'Volunteering lies at the very heart of ADS and all our volunteers play a key role in the work we do. With the help of hundreds of volunteers each day we are able to reach out and help more people than ever before. We have a rich and diverse pool of volunteers in the heart of all the communities in which we work. There are a variety of volunteering opportunities and roles which you can look at below. If volunteering with us sounds like something you could do then please do get in touch we would love to hear from you. We offer a superb training package and will cover your expenses'.

Elderly Health and Care

Age UK

www.ageuk.org.uk
contact@ageuk.org.uk
Tel: 0800 169 6565
'Age UK has a vision of a world in which older people flourish. We aim to improve later life for everyone through our information and advice, campaigns, products, training and research'. With Age UK you can volunteer in one of their 470 shops, get involved with your local community, help out at their London office, or join a committee.

Alzheimer's Society

www.alzheimers.org.uk
enquiries@alzheimers.org.uk
Tel: 020 7423 3500
'Alzheimer's Society is a membership organisation, which works to improve the quality of life of people affected by dementia in England, Wales and Northern Ireland. Many of our 25,000 members have personal experience of dementia, as carers, health professionals or people with dementia themselves, and their experiences help to inform our work. Volunteering is flexible, ranging from a few hours a year to several hours a week. It's your choice. Volunteers help us deliver local services, in our areas, in the regional and country offices, as well as at our central office in London'.

WRVS

www.wrvs.org.uk

Tel: 0845 600 5885

'WRVS is an age-positive national charity founded over 70 years ago. We believe that every older person should have the opportunity and choice to get more out of life.

'Around 45,000 dedicated volunteers deliver services that help older people live the life they want to. They make a massive difference within their communities and are committed to making Britain a great place to grow old. Whether it's taking an older person to the shops, delivering a meal to them or even walking their dog – you can make a big difference that is appreciated and valued'.

Carers

Carers UK

www.carersuk.org

Tel: 0808 808 7777

'Carers UK is a charity set up to help the millions of people who care for family or friends. Carers UK has a local network of around 60 branches run by volunteers. Our branches are a way for carers and former carers to support each other, share information and advice and campaign for change. Some of our branches provide telephone helplines, sitting services, support groups, activities and days out. Others focus on being a local voice for carers, working with councils, trusts and hospitals to address issues that concern carers. Sadly, our branch network doesn't cover everywhere. You can find out if there is a branch near you by searching on our website'.

Crossroads

www.crossroads.org.uk

Tel: 0845 450 0350

'Crossroads Care is Britain's leading provider of support for carers and the people they care for. We work with over 41,000 individuals and their families, helping carers make a life of their own outside caring.

'The contribution of volunteers is essential to the success of Crossroads Care. Our local Crossroads Care charities have the valuable support of volunteers in a range of roles'.

Women and girls

Refuge

www.refuge.org.uk
volunteering@refuge.org.uk
Tel: 020 7395 7700
'We believe that every woman and child experiencing domestic violence has different needs – there is no single package of services to meet those needs, no "one size fits all". Refuge offers a range of services which gives women and children access to professional support whatever their situation.
'Refuge relies on the goodwill of dedicated individuals to continue its fight against domestic violence. If you can spare an hour a month or a few hours a year, you can become part of a greater family, striving for a world free from violence. We value your time and aim to make best possible use of your skills'.

Criminal Justice System

Victim Support

www.victimsupport.org.uk
Tel: 0800 840 4207 (national volunteering line)
A national charity giving free and confidential help to victims of crime, witnesses, their family, friends and anyone else affected across England and Wales. They also speak out as a national voice for victims and witnesses and campaign for change.

Independent Custody Visiting Association (ICVA)

http://www.icva.org.uk/
info@icva.org.uk
The Independent Custody Visiting Association is a voluntary organisation that promotes and supports the effective provision of custody visiting nationally, raising public awareness on the rights and entitlements, health and wellbeing of people held in police custody and the conditions and facilities in which they are kept. Independent custody visitors check on the standards in which people are held in custody, enhancing the accountability and transparency of police among the communities they serve. Visitors play a vital role in raising standards in custody and the fair treatment of detainees.
If you are interested in becoming an Independent Custody Visitor in your area, please contact your local police authority.

Prison Advice and Care Trust (pact)

www.prisonadvice.org.uk
volunteers@prisonadvice.org.uk
Tel: 020 7735 9535
'The Prison Advice & Care Trust (pact) is a charity which supports people affected by imprisonment. We provide practical and emotional support to prisoners' children and families, and to prisoners themselves.
'Could you volunteer for pact? We are always seeking volunteers to help out at our projects across the country'.

Adult Education

Workers' Educational Association (WEA)

www.wea.org.uk
'The Workers' Educational Association (WEA) is the UK's largest voluntary sector provider of adult education. We provide around 12,000 part-time courses each year, reaching over 80,000 adults of all ages and educational backgrounds. We operate in all nine English regions and in Scotland.

'Currently, we have over one thousand volunteers actively involved in our work. Our volunteer roles are varied, and differ by location and branch, depending on local need. Volunteers help to arrange local courses, promote and publicise courses, join governance committees and carry out a range of tasks from administration to running local events'.

Youth and Young People

The Prince's Trust

www.princes-trust.org.uk
webinfops@princes-trust.org.uk
Tel: 020 7543 1234 (Head Office)
'The Prince's Trust operates from 12 national and regional offices in the UK. The Prince's Trust is the UK's leading youth charity offering 14-to 30-year-olds opportunities to develop confidence, learn new skills, get into work and start businesses. The Prince's Trust targets those not in education, employment or training; young offenders; and those in or leaving care.
'We have volunteering roles in a variety of shapes and sizes. Volunteers have a powerful influence on the success of our programmes, and on the young people they help'.

Sport

English Federation of Disability Sport (EFDS)

www.efds.co.uk
Tel: 01509 227 750.
'English Federation of Disability Sport (EFDS) is the national body responsible for developing sport for disabled people in England. As a registered charity we rely on funding to support our work. Working with key partners, including National Disability Sport Organisations (NDSOs), we aim to increase and improve sports opportunities.

'Volunteers are the life blood of sport. Without volunteers, sport for disabled people would not exist. EFDS is committed to getting more disabled people involved in sport and physical activity as participants and volunteers. Even if you can only spare a few hours, it really does make all the difference.'

Animals

Hearing Dogs for Deaf People

www.hearingdogs.org.uk
volunteer@hearingdogs.org.uk.
Tel: 01759 322299
'We train hearing dogs to alert deaf people to select household sounds and danger signals in the home, workplace and in public buildings – providing a life-changing level of independence, confidence and security.
Hearing Dogs' volunteers are the lifeline of the charity. Without the tireless support of our volunteers across a wide range of roles, we would not be able to provide so many life-changing hearing dogs to deaf recipients'.

The Blue Cross

www.bluecross.org.uk
info@bluecross.org.uk
Tel: 0300 777 1897
'We are a charity dedicated to improving the lives of sick and unwanted pets. At The Blue Cross we take in animals of all shapes and sizes, from hamsters to horses, and we find them loving new homes. We make sure thousands more get the veterinary treatment they need when their owners cannot afford to pay. Our volunteers undertake a wide range of roles, from working directly with animals, working on reception and admin, helping out in our charity shops; and helping us with fundraising and events. We also have three national volunteering projects, our educational speaker programme, our pet bereavement support helpline, and our rehoming foster scheme'.

Arts

Create Arts

www.createarts.org.uk
www.voluntaryarts.org.uk
sabita@createarts.org.uk
Tel: 020 7374 8485
'Create uses the creative arts to help transform the lives of the most disadvantaged and vulnerable people in our society. We do this by engaging leading professional artists across a wide range of art forms that can inspire, encourage and motivate people of all ages to explore their creativity, develop life skills, become more self-confident and have fun!'

Environment, Heritage and Conservation

BTCV

www2.btcv.org.uk
information@btcv.org.uk
Tel: 01302 388 883
Established in 1959, BTCV is one of the largest environmental volunteering organisations in the UK. BTCV enables people to make in a difference in their lives and improve the places around them. The charity supports hundreds of thousands of people to think and act differently to improve their environment every year on projects both here in the UK and abroad. BTCV works with 628,000 volunteers a year.

National Trust

www.nationaltrust.org.uk
volunteers@nationaltrust.org.uk
Tel: 01793 817632

'The National Trust is a charity and is completely independent of government. We rely for income on membership fees, donations and legacies, and revenue raised from our commercial operations. We have over 3.6 million members and 55,000 volunteers. More than 14 million people visit our pay for entry properties, while an estimated 50 million visit our open air properties.

'We protect and open to the public over 350 historic houses, gardens and ancient monuments. But it doesn't stop there. We also look after forests, woods, fens, beaches, farmland, downs, moorland, islands, archaeological remains, castles, nature reserves, villages – forever, for everyone.

'Looking for an exciting and interesting way to make a difference in conserving the environment and the UK's heritage? Whatever your interests or skills, we would love to hear from you.'

Other Useful Organisations

Volunteering England

www.volunteering.org.uk
volunteering@volunteeringengland.org

Volunteering England is a national volunteer development organisation for England. It works across the voluntary, public and private sectors to raise the profile of volunteering as a force for change. Contact details for your nearest Volunteer Centre can be found on the Volunteering England website.

If you live in Scotland go to www.volunteerscotland.org.uk

If you live in Ireland go to www.volunteer.ie

Wales Council for Voluntary Action (WCVA)

www.wcva.org.uk
help@wcva.org.uk
Tel: 0800 2888 329
WCVA is the voice of the voluntary sector in Wales, representing and campaigning for voluntary organisations, volunteers and communities.

Do-it.org.uk (YouthNet UK)

www.do-it.org.uk
Do-it is an Internet database of volunteering opportunities, and covers the whole UK. The database can be searched by postcode, type of volunteering activity and type of organisation.

TimeBank

www.timebank.org.uk
TimeBank is a national charity that provides people with the inspiration, opportunities and support to volunteer. It was created for those who know their time and skills are in demand, but do not know where to begin.
TimeBank constantly develops new, exciting ways to involve volunteers and its projects address very real needs. People who register with TimeBank have access to an online chat forum where they can get all their volunteering questions answered.
Go to www.timebank.org.uk and enter your postcode to find out about volunteering opportunities near you.

DirectGov

www.direct.gov.uk
The DirectGov website offers a wealth of information on volunteering and related issues in the 'Home and Community' section.

CSV

www.csv.org.uk
information@csv.org.uk
For projects in England, call 020 7278 6601
For projects in Wales, call 02920 415 700
For projects in Scotland, call 0131 622 7766
'Founded in 1962, CSV is the UK's leading volunteering and training charity. CSV's vision is of a society where everyone can participate to build healthy, enterprising, inclusive communities. Every year, CSV involves over 150,000 volunteers in high quality opportunities that enrich lives and tackle real need. Between them, they help transform the lives of over 1 million people across the UK
'CSV volunteers come from all age groups and all walks of life. They touch the lives of over a million people across the UK each year. At the core of what we do is the belief that anyone can be a volunteer no matter who they are or where they come from. We reject no one'.

Worldwide Volunteering

www.wwv.org.uk
Tel: 01935 825588
Established as a charity in 1994, WorldWide Volunteering helps people of all ages to take part in fulfilling and inspiring volunteering projects in the UK and around the world.

Skills-based volunteering: Reach

www.reachskills.org.uk
Tel: 020 7582 6543
Reach is a charity which recruits people of all ages and backgrounds throughout the UK with specific business, professional, managerial or technical career experience and finds them part-time, expenses only opportunities, with voluntary organisations which need their expertise.

Older people's volunteering:

RSVP (Retired and Senior Volunteer Programme)

www.csv-rsvp.org.uk

This programme is run by CSV, and offers the opportunity for everyone over the age of 50 to volunteer.

Young people: V

www.vinspired.com

V can advise you on finding volunteering opportunities if you are aged 16-25.

GuideStar UK

www.guidestar.org.uk

The GuideStar website contains information on approximately 168,000 registered charities in England and Wales, so can be used to find local groups in your area. Once you've identified the voluntary groups that you'd like to volunteer with, you can contact them directly to find out what sort of volunteering opportunities they have available.

References

Ellis Paine, A, Hill, M & Rochester C, *A rose by any other name . . . Revisiting the question: 'what exactly is volunteering?'* Working paper series: Paper one, Institute of Volunteering Research 2010
Volunteering and Health: What impact does it really have? Volunteer England 2008
Making the case for volunteering Volunteering England Impact Report 2010

Bibliography

Rochester, C, Ellis Paine, A, Howlett, S with Zimmeck, M, *Volunteering and Society in the 21st Century*, Palgrave Macmillan, 2010.

Volunteering Compact and Code of Good Practice, Home Office, London, 2005

The Guardian Guide to Volunteering (Guardian Books 2007)

Volunteering England Information Sheet: *Thinking about volunteering?* Volunteering England 2011(available for free from www.volunteering.org.uk)

Volunteering England Information Sheet: *Who is allowed to volunteer?* Volunteering England 2011(available for free from www.volunteering.org.uk)

Volunteering England Information Sheet: *Finding volunteering opportunities* Volunteering England 2011(available for free from www.volunteering.org.uk)

Volunteering England Information Sheet: *Residential Volunteering Opportunities in the UK* Volunteering England, 2009, (available for free from www.volunteering.org.uk)

Volunteering England Information Sheet: *Volunteering outside the UK* Volunteering England 2011(available for free from www.volunteering.org.uk)

Volunteering England Information Sheet: *Accreditation of Volunteering* Volunteering England 2009 (available for free from www.volunteering.org.uk)

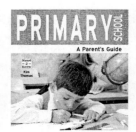

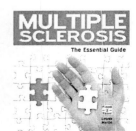